Your First QUILT BOOK

(or it should be!)

Carol Doak

That Patchwork Place

Credits

Editor-in-Chief	Kerry I. Smith
Technical Editor	Ursula Reikes
Managing Editor	Judy Petry
Design Director	Cheryl Stevenson
Cover Designer	Cheryl Stevenson
Text Designer	Amy Shayne
Design Assistant	Keather Weideman
Production Assistant	Marge Mueller
Copy Editor	Liz McGehee
Proofreader	Leslie Phillips
Illustrator	Laurel Strand
Decorative Art	Nicki Salvin-Wight
Photographer	Brent Kane

Your First Quilt Book (or it should be!)
© 1997 by Carol Doak
Martingale & Company
20205 144th Avenue NE, Woodinville, WA 98072
Printed in USA
ISBN 0-7394-3453-5

MISSION STATEMENT

WE ARE DEDICATED TO PROVIDING QUALITY PRODUCTS AND SERVICE BY WORKING TOGETHER TO INSPIRE CREATIVITY AND TO ENRICH THE LIVES WE TOUCH.

Dedication

This book is dedicated to Ursula Reikes, who was introduced to me as an editor and remains in my heart as a very dear friend.

Acknowledgments

Writing a book such as this does not happen without lots of encouragement and support from friends and family. I would like to extend my heartfelt hugs and appreciation to:

My dear friend, Sherry Reis, for being my constant cheerleader;

My quilting buddies, Moira Clegg, Beth Meek, Terry Maddox, Ginny Guaraldi, Mary Kay Sieve, Peggy Forand, Pam Ludwig, and Judy Kelly for their support and for overlooking the dust when quilting was at my house;

Ellen Peters for her exquisite machine quilting, creative quilting designs, and machine-quilting tips;

My husband, Alan, for being my personal computer tech, and my son, Jeff, for offering to cook dinner when I was writing;

Each and every delightful person at That Patchwork Place who makes writing books such a joy.

Table of Contents

Preface

I wish I had a nickel for each time someone gazed at one of my quilts and said, "Oh, I would never have the patience to do that." In reality, there is no patience required to do something you enjoy. Quilters make quilts because they enjoy the process of choosing or designing a project. They enjoy the process of selecting their fabrics and the satisfaction of creating something unique and special.

You are probably reading this book because you want to learn about patchwork and quilting, and perhaps you are a bit overwhelmed. You might even fall into the "I haven't got a clue" category. Maybe you know someone who makes quilts and have heard them speak in a foreign tongue, using terms like "half-square triangles," "betweens," and "fat quarters." Perhaps you wandered into a quilt shop and gazed at thousands of bolts of fabric and walked out with your head spinning. On the other hand, maybe you are the adventurous type and started a quilt only to discover there must be more to this than meets the eye. You are a beginning quilter!

My purpose in writing *Your First Quilt Book (or it should be!)* is to provide you with information about the tools, supplies, and techniques for your first pieced patchwork projects in a simple, conversational, and fun way. Your first quilting experiences should be enjoyable and a time of discovery. I tried to contain myself and provide only information that will lay a good foundation for understanding patchwork and quilting. The entire scope of quiltmaking is not covered in this book. When you are ready to learn more about a particular subject matter, you can find more detailed information in the books suggested on page 221.

I have been quilting for more than seventeen years, and I am still learning and making discoveries. Your first project need not be a hand-pieced and hand-quilted king-size quilt. You can learn and experience a variety of pieced patchwork skills through small projects. The projects in this book range in scope from a one-block pillow to a lap quilt using several blocks. Begin at the level where you feel most comfortable. Step-by-step hand-piecing and machine-piecing directions are provided for all the projects. Each quilting project provides experience and knowledge to build on and use in subsequent projects.

Some patchwork and quilting skills are easy to achieve when you use the appropriate methods and materials. Other techniques require practice to reach the desired skill level. The old adage "the more you do, the better you get" applies to these acquired-skill techniques.

Welcome to the art of quiltmaking. As you work through *Your First Quilt Book,* consider our gal as your personal quilting teacher. She is ready to lend a helping hand, instill confidence along the way, and keep it fun (this is, after all, not brain surgery). May your first experiences and those down the road be rewarding and enjoyable.

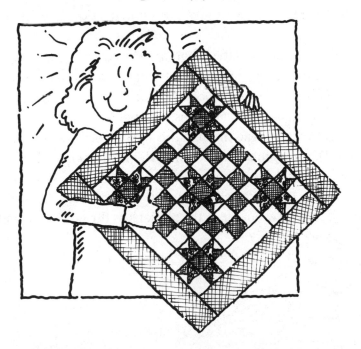

Introduction

Perhaps you've always dreamed of creating your own patchwork quilts but never knew where to start. This book was written just for you! It will provide basic information in a friendly, reassuring style with lots of illustrations and a bit of humor to keep the learning easy and fun. The patchwork projects are small and designed not to overwhelm.

Descriptions, functions, and pictures of basic quiltmaking tools are contained in the "Tools and Supplies" chapter. Now you know what to add to your gift list this year!

The "Pieced-Patchwork Block Designs" chapter explains the origins of many traditional patchwork block designs. This information will not only help you during the patchwork process, but will also be invaluable when you are ready to create your own patchwork designs.

The "Pieced-Patchwork Techniques" chapter explores the difference between working by hand or by machine. It provides you with a bit of insight so you can decide whether to make your first project by hand, by machine, or a combination of both. You will not be considered an evil person if you pursue machine patchwork and machine quilting. They are both quite acceptable. It simply comes down to your preferred method of work. If you enjoy the process, you will find the time to work on your project and will be more likely to complete it.

The small projects in the "Beginner Projects" chapter are geared just for the beginner so you can jump right in and try handwork, machine work, or both. The remaining chapters will provide the necessary information to assemble, quilt, and finish your projects.

You will want to read through this book to become familiar with the concepts. Don't try to remember everything. There is no test. Think of it as a trusty reference you can turn to time and again. However, a read-through will provide you with the whole picture. Then, as you create your projects, you can refer to the sections in the book that apply.

As you read, you'll see some symbols alongside the text. Here is what they mean:

Tip boxes include handy hints that will make a process or technique a bit easier. Read these right away!

Alert boxes will let you know when you need to be careful. Your guardian angel will alert you so you don't make a common mistake.

Down the Road boxes contain information that will come in handy on future patchwork projects, after you have some quilt-making experience. You don't need this information right away, though, so feel free to ignore the Down the Road boxes until you're ready to explore a bit more.

I know that venturing into unfamiliar areas can be uncomfortable. I kept this in mind as I wrote this book and created these projects. I have every confidence that you will be successful and find enjoyment making these patchwork projects that are designed specifically for a beginning quilter.

Quilting-Language Translations

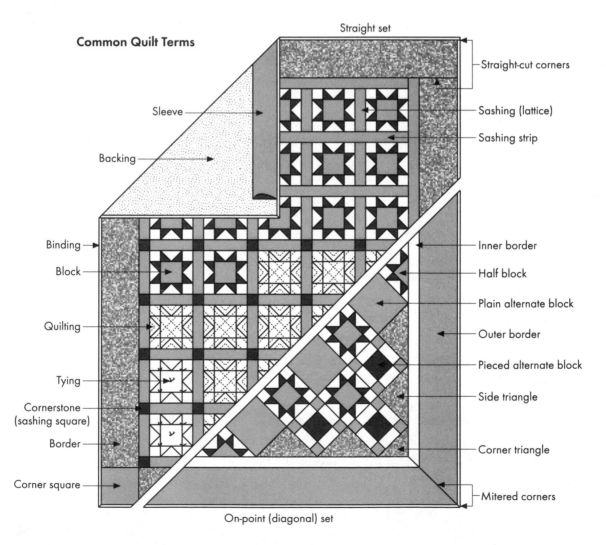

Common Quilt Terms

Straight set

Straight-cut corners

Sleeve

Sashing (lattice)

Sashing strip

Backing

Binding

Inner border

Block

Half block

Plain alternate block

Quilting

Outer border

Tying

Pieced alternate block

Side triangle

Cornerstone
(sashing square)

Border

Corner triangle

Corner square

Mitered corners

On-point (diagonal) set

Quilters really don't speak a foreign language, but you are likely to read or hear terms that are unfamiliar. The following terms are common in the world of quilters.

Alternate Blocks: Secondary blocks that alternate with the main blocks in a quilt. They can be pieced, appliquéd, or plain.

Appliqué: A technique in which fabric shapes are sewn on top of other pieces of fabric. Since we had to limit the focus of this beginner book, you will need to refer to other sources for appliqué techniques. See "Suggested Books" on page 221.

Backing: The bottom layer of the quilt.

Backstitch: Two stitches taken in the same place when sewing a running stitch.

Basting: Long running stitches to temporarily hold fabric in place.

Batting: The middle layer of the quilt (the part that makes the quilt warm and the quilting designs puffy).

Bearding: Batting fibers that work their way through to the top of the quilt. (This is not a good thing! See page 182.)

Betweens: Needles used for the quilting process (sewing the three layers together).

Bias Grain: The fabric grain that runs at a 45° angle. Fabric has the greatest amount of stretch there.

Binding: A finishing treatment for the edge of a quilt project.

Bleeding: Don't run for the Band-Aids. It's when the color from one fabric transfers to another fabric when washed.

Block: A unit created when you sew patches together. These can be pieced or appliquéd.

Borders: Strips of fabric that frame the blocks in a quilt. They can be one piece of fabric or pieced patchwork.

Chain Piecing: A process where patches are machine sewn consecutively without cutting the thread. Also called *fast feeding*.

Continuous-Line Quilting: A quilting design in which the design line keeps on going so you don't have to stop and start in different places.

Corner Square: A square that fills the corner of a border.

Corner Triangles: The four triangles placed in the corners of a diagonally set quilt (on-point). These are half-square triangles, and the straight grain is on the short sides of the triangles.

Cornerstones: Squares of fabric used to join sashing strips where they intersect. Also called *sashing squares*.

Even-Feed Foot: *See* Walking Foot.

Fast Feeding: *See* Chain Piecing.

Fat Eighth: A piece of fabric that measures 9" x 22".

Fat Quarter: A piece of fabric that measures 18" x 22".

Feed Dogs: The teethlike mechanism under the presser foot of your sewing machine that moves the fabric along as you stitch.

Finger Pressing: Letting your fingers do the walking (walking your fingers along the fabric seam to crease it).

Half-Square Triangles: The triangles created when a square is cut once diagonally from corner to corner. The straight grain is on the short sides of the triangles.

In-the-Ditch: A kind of straight-line quilting where you stitch right next to a seam where there is no seam allowance.

Lattice: *See* Sashing.

Long Darners (size 7): Long, thin needles used when basting a quilt.

Mitered-Corner Borders: Borders where the corner seams are sewn at a 45° angle. In our effort to narrow the focus of this book to a couple of options, we are not addressing mitered corners.

On-point: A block placed diagonally at a 45° angle within the quilt top.

Piecing: The process of sewing patches of fabric together.

Quarter-Square Triangles: The triangles created when a square is cut twice diagonally from corner to corner. The straight grain is on the long side of the triangles.

Quilt-As-You-Go: A method where the quilt is sewn in sections, including quilting the three layers together, before joining them.

Quilt Challenge: Several people making a quilting project within certain predetermined criteria.

Quilt Frame: A small hand-held frame or a large floor frame that holds the quilt layers during the quilting process.

Quilt Hoop: Two circles (or ovals, squares, rectangles) that hold the quilt layers during the quilting process.

Quilt Label: A patch sewn to the back of a quilt providing information about the quilt, its maker, and the recipient.

Quilt Sandwich: The three layers of a quilt: the quilt top, the batting, and the backing.

Quilt Sleeve: A strip of fabric attached to the back of the quilt during the finishing stage so a rod can be slipped inside to hang the quilt.

Quilting: The process of sewing the three quilt layers together, using a hand running stitch or the sewing machine. Also used to describe the technique of making quilts.

Quilting Thread: A sturdy thread used to hand quilt the three layers together. It will say "quilting thread" on the spool.

Rocker Quilting Stitch: A method of quilting (sewing the three layers together) where a needle is rocked back and forth through the three layers in a running stitch.

Rotary Cutter: A cutting tool that has a round razorlike blade (like a pizza cutter).

Rotary Mat: A surface made for cutting fabric with the rotary cutter.

Rotary Rulers: Thick, see-through plastic rulers for use with the rotary cutter.

Running Stitch: A method of sewing where the needle goes in and out of the fabric in a continuous motion.

Sandpaper Marking Board: A piece of fine sandpaper attached to a board. It is helpful when marking fabric because it grabs the fabric and holds it in place.

Sashing: Strips of fabric sewn between the blocks of a quilt. Also called *lattice*.

Sashing Squares: *See* Cornerstones.

Scrap Quilts: Quilts that use a large number of different fabrics.

Seam Allowance: The extra fabric on the other side of the sewing line. The standard patchwork seam allowance is ¼" on all sides of each patchwork shape.

Selvages: The manufactured finished edges of fabric.

Setting: The arrangement of blocks and other fabric pieces in a quilt. A straight setting is where the blocks are placed in a vertical and horizontal grid fashion. A diagonal setting is where they are placed on-point.

Sharps: Sewing needles used for hand piecing or appliqué.

Side Triangles: The setting triangles placed on the sides, top, and bottom of a diagonally set quilt (on-point) to fill it out. These are quarter-square triangles, and the straight grain is on the long side of the triangles.

Stab Stitching: A method of hand quilting where the needle is pushed to the underside of the quilt with one hand and returned to the top with the other hand.

Stencils: Cutout designs used for marking quilting designs on the quilt top.

Straight-Cut Borders: Top, bottom, and side borders that meet at a horizontal seam.

Straight Grain: The grain that runs vertically (lengthwise grain) and horizontally (crosswise grain) through the fabric.

Strip Piecing: A process where strips of fabric are sewn together, cut into segments, and resewn one or more times to create patchwork.

Template: A patchwork shape that is placed on the fabric and used as a pattern to trace or cut around. Your templates can be the finished size of the shape or the size of the shape plus seam allowances, depending upon whether you are hand or machine piecing.

Thimble: A protective covering for your finger used during the hand sewing and quilting processes.

Tied Quilt: A quilt that has the three layers secured with thread or yarn knotted at regular intervals instead of quilting stitches. See pages 198–99.

Walking Foot: A presser-foot attachment that feeds two or more layers through at the same rate. Also called *even-feed foot.*

Fabrics, Fabrics, Fabrics

"She who dies with the most fabric wins!"

Quilters have a real love affair with fabrics and have even coined phrases like "She who dies with the most fabric wins!" If you have been purchasing fabrics and creating a "fabric stash," you are a budding quilter about to bloom. Although other types of fabric may be incorporated into your projects later, I suggest you start with 100% cotton woven fabric. The cotton will be easier to work with and will crease along the patchwork lines more easily than other types of fabric.

If you used only white solid fabrics in your fabric patches, you would have no patchwork design at all. It is the combination of value, texture, and color in fabric that creates a design. Quiltmaking is a creative activity. Many of the decisions you make along the way, including picking out your fabrics, are expressions of your creativity. There is no right and wrong choice, only your choice. It is your quilt and your decision.

Looking at Fabric Graphics

Value: The Light and Dark of It!

Value is not how much a fabric is worth, but the lightness or darkness of the color. A black-and-white photograph shows only value. To make your patchwork designs visible, you need to use a variety of values to create contrast. The higher the contrast, the more graphic the patchwork design will be. Conversely, the lower the contrast, the more subtle the patchwork design will be. You can change the look of a design by changing the placement and number of values used.

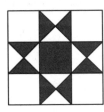 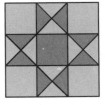 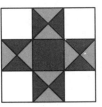 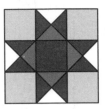

High Contrast   Low Contrast   Three Values   Four Values

Different value placement creates different designs.

Keep in mind that the value of a certain fabric depends on what surrounds it. A medium-value fabric looks light when placed next to a dark-value fabric, and dark when placed next to a light-value fabric.

The center squares in both these block designs are exactly the same value, but this value appears light in the first block and dark in the second block.

It's not always easy to decide whether one fabric is lighter or darker than another when you are looking at many different-colored fabrics. To help you determine the values in a group of fabrics, look at the whole group through a see-through, red-tinted piece of plastic, such as a Ruby Beholder®. This helpful tool eliminates the color in the fabric; what remains is the value: light, medium, or dark. It does not, however, work well with fabrics in the red color family.

Fabrics are available in an abundance of large- and small-scale florals, geometric prints, swirls, stripes, and solids. For the beginning quilter, combining several prints in one project can be an uncomfortable task. Thus far, your only experience with prints may have been in clothing, where a variety of prints is considered a no-no. Well, this variety does work in patchwork, partly because it is tradition and partly because the prints used in the blocks add texture to a design. When combining textures, strive for a variety that enhances each other.

Textures: Variety and Camouflage

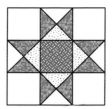

Prints add texture to your patchwork.

One way to get a handle on the variety of textures is to categorize them.

Solid Fabrics: Fabrics that are a single color with no design or print at all.

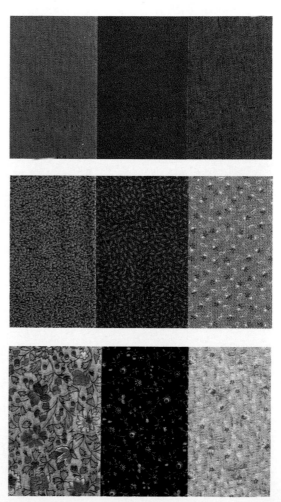

Mini-Print Fabrics: Tiny-scale fabrics that usually contain a limited number of colors. Intricate quilting designs will show up nicely, without sending out radar signals about possible uneven stitches. A mismatched seam will be camouflaged! This concealing capability is an advantage for beginners who are learning and perfecting their skills.

Calico Fabrics: Small-scale prints typically seen in traditional patchwork. These fabrics often contain several colors.

Dot Fabrics: Fabrics with a single element that looks like a polka dot. This is a different texture that will add interest to your patchwork.

Airy Fabrics: Fabrics that have a quiet background with subtle line designs. Often, only a few colors are used.

Large-Scale Fabrics: Fabrics with large elements in the design. There are often many colors in large-scale prints. They can set the theme for your project when used in large pieces. When a large-scale print is cut up in small pieces, the design itself may not be evident, and you end up with splashes of color throughout the patchwork.

Stripe Fabrics: Fabrics that contain small-scale stripes, large-scale stripes, or both within the same fabric. Stripe fabrics make it look like you worked harder than you did because they often make the patchwork appear pieced. They also tend to lead the eye in a particular direction.

Geometric Fabrics: Fabrics with straight lines that create geometric patterns.

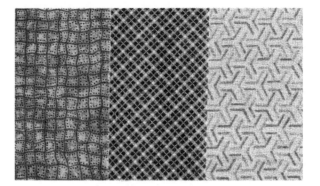

Some things to consider when choosing fabrics:

- Solid fabrics might seem like a safe choice for a beginner who is struggling with combining a variety of prints. They are not, however, nearly as forgiving as prints in hiding slight imperfections in your beginning patchwork and quilting.

- When selecting calicoes, be sure you stand back to see what colors dominate in these fabrics. Although there may be many colors in the fabric, only a few colors will stand out in your patchwork.

- Although dots offer another texture, avoid using a lot of fabrics with this type of single element in the same project. It will make it difficult for your eyes to focus on the overall design.

Tone-on-Tone Fabrics: Prints with only one color but with different values of that color. Although the scale and type of print can vary, these subtle prints offer a quiet change of pace.

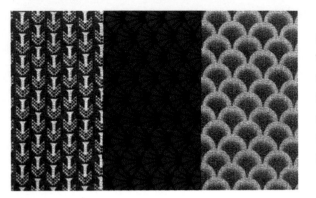

Directional Fabrics: Fabrics that have a definite direction to their design. An example would be a fabric with apples all facing in the same direction. It may drive you crazy if some of the apples get turned upside down or sideways during piecing, so you may want to avoid these fabrics for awhile. As a beginner, you don't need another thing to worry about.

The wrong side of the fabric can sometimes be used as the right side. Remember, you bought and paid for both sides of the fabric!

Color: So Many Choices, So Little Time

The best advice I can give you is to choose colors you like and will enjoy handling. You can make a project using just one color in a variety of values. You can combine a warm color (red, orange, yellow) and a cool color (blue, green, lavender) for a nice effect. You can combine your favorite colors or the colors in your room decor for a wall quilt.

Take your inspiration for combining colors in a project from one print that you really like. Calicoes and large-scale prints often contain many colors. Select the remainder of the fabrics for your project from the colors in that one fabric. You don't need to visualize how the colors will work together because you can see them in the fabric.

Keep in mind the following when choosing fabrics for your quilt.

Light-colored areas appear larger than dark-colored areas. If you want to make an area of patchwork appear smaller, a darker fabric will do the trick. And conversely, if you want to highlight an area of patchwork and make it appear larger, use a lighter fabric.

Warm colors appear to come forward and cool colors appear to recede. Warm colors are associated with fire, such as red, orange, and yellow. Cool colors are associated with water and grass, such as blue and green.

A fabric with high contrast does not blend easily with other fabrics. When you try to place this type of fabric in a group of fabrics by value, it looks too light when placed with the darker fabrics and too dark when placed with the lighter fabrics. In the example below, the fabrics in the first group appear to blend. In the second group, the green and white fabric, which has a high contrast, appears too light for the dark fabrics and too dark for the light fabrics.

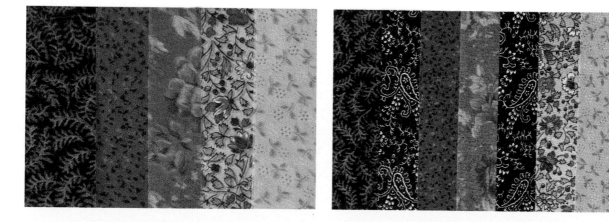

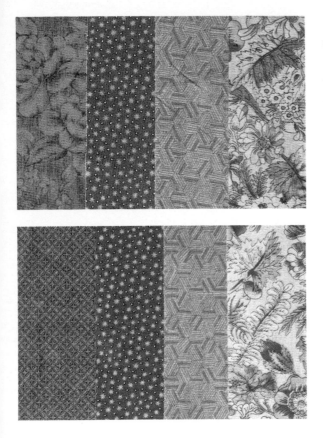

Using colors with the same intensity creates a pleasant balance. Intensity is the brightness or dullness in the color. For instance, if you are making a baby quilt using soft pastels, you wouldn't want to include a day-glow yellow. Those areas would pop off the quilt and make the child cross-eyed! On the other hand, a soft pastel yellow would look washed out in a strong red and blue quilt. In the example at left, the green in the first group (top) is too intense for the colors in the other fabrics. The green in the second group (bottom) works better because it is similar in intensity. Trust me, you don't need to agonize over this. Usually a fabric that is too intense sends out radar signals immediately.

Adding just a bit of a much darker fabric will provide spark and interest to your project. The medium purple in the first patchwork block works OK, but the much darker purple in the second patchwork block adds a bit of "punch" to the block.

Selecting Fabric without Stress

Once you have determined how many different values, colors, and textures you want, you are ready to buy your fabric. If you are lucky enough to have a quilt shop in your area, you will more than likely find it to be a nurturing and friendly environment. It can be overwhelming walking into a store and seeing thousands of bolts of fabric staring back at you, but you can handle this! You just need to cut the task down to size. Fortunately, fabrics are usually grouped by color so you can march over to the color you're looking for and select your favorite print in the value you want.

Look for different textures to add interest and variety to your quilt. A quilt of all calicoes is not as interesting as a quilt that contains a variety of textures. You don't need one of each texture type; you just want a nice variety so your patchwork will have interest without looking busy.

Stack the bolts flat so you are looking at the edge of the bolts, and step back about ten feet to gain a better perspective of how the fabrics will work together in your quilt. The fabric group at right contains variety in color, value, and texture.

How Much Fabric Should I Buy? (you'll love this answer!)

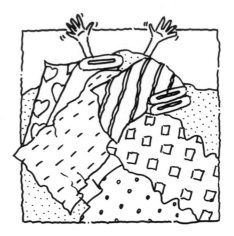

All of it! Just kidding. Seriously, many quilters buy fabric they like when they see it, so they'll have it on hand for future projects. This is called building a fabric stash. It really isn't such a bad idea, since fabrics change quickly on the shelves, and what you see this season probably won't be there next season. Consider the following guidelines:

If you like it, buy a yard.
If you really like it, buy 2 yards.
If you can't live without it, buy as much as your budget permits.

A more logical approach would be to consider the size of your future projects. If you expect to work on small quilts, 1 to 2 yards would be a reasonable amount. If you expect to work on large bed-size quilts, 3 or 4 yards would make sense.

Estimating Yardage

Yardage requirements are provided for all the projects in this book. However, if you are planning your own project, you can estimate or calculate how much fabric is needed. If you are working on a small project and don't mind having a bit of extra fabric around for future use, generously estimate your needs. If your finished project is 36" x 36" and you are using three different fabrics in similar amounts, then ½ yard of each fabric is plenty. That gives you 1½ yards of fabric to make a project that is approximately 1 yard in size. You will need more than what is seen in the patchwork to allow for the seam allowances. Unlike other sewing projects where extra fabric is often never used, extra fabric can always be used in future scrap quilts. It may be just the perfect fabric for a future project.

You can also use the "longest-piece" method to estimate yardage. Suppose you are making a project that will finish to 50" square, with a 4"-wide straight-cut border. Since the top and bottom borders are the longest pieces, you will need to cut 2 strips that are 4½" x 50½". (Remember the standard seam allowance for patchwork is ¼" on all sides.) Cotton fabric is approximately 44" wide; therefore, the 2 strips must be cut along the length of the fabric because they're too long to fit across the width. That means, you need a piece of fabric at least 50½" long.

Since you would never buy exactly what you need for length, round up to the nearest fraction of a yard. One yard (36") plus a half yard (18") equals 54". Only 18" of that 1½ yards will be used for the borders (four times 4½" equals 18"), so the remainder will be available for other parts of the quilt or future projects.

The following chart lists fabric yardage and the size of the piece in inches.

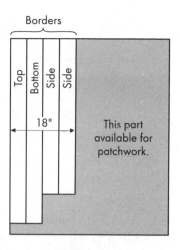

Borders

Top / Bottom / Side / Side

18"

This part available for patchwork.

Helpful Yardage Chart

YARDAGE	SIZE OF FABRIC PIECE	YARDAGE	SIZE OF FABRIC PIECE
⅛ yd.	4½" x 44"*	⅝ yd.	22½" x 44"
¼ yd.	9" x 44"*	⅔ yd.	24" x 44"
⅓ yd.	12" x 44"	¾ yd.	27" x 44"
⅜ yd.	13½" x 44"	⅞ yd.	31½" x 44"
½ yd.	18" x 44"	1 yd.	36" x 44"

*A common term in patchwork is "fat quarter." A fat quarter is one-quarter of a yard of fabric that is made by cutting ½ yard of fabric (18" x 44") and then cutting it vertically in the middle (22"), making a one-quarter-yard piece that is 18" x 22". A "fat eighth" is cut in a similar manner and measures 9" x 22".

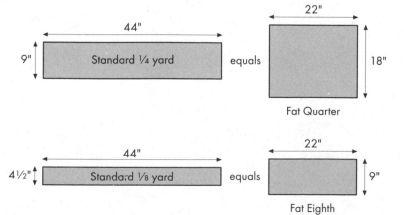

44"

9" Standard ¼ yard   equals

22"

18"

Fat Quarter

44"

4½" Standard ⅛ yard   equals

22"

9"

Fat Eighth

Calculating Yardage

Sometimes, you may want to calculate how much fabric you need for your patchwork. By the way, I use a calculator to do any "calculations." First, determine the cut size of each patch (the size of the patch plus ½" total for seam allowances) and the number needed for your project. Suppose you are making a quilt of 12 patchwork blocks, and there are 5 rectangles in each block that are 3½" x 5½" finished. You will need 60 rectangles, each 4" x 6" (3½" + ½" = 4" and 5½" + ½" = 6"). Or, suppose you are making a quilt that requires 60 appliqué rabbits that are cut 4" wide and 6" tall (see definition of "appliqué" on page 11). You only have one yard of wonderful rabbit fabric, and before you mark and cut out all those rabbits, you want to make sure you will have enough fabric. (OK, I realize that we aren't going to cover appliqué in this book, but the rabbit example will be more fun to describe, and the yardage calculations will be the same for both examples.)

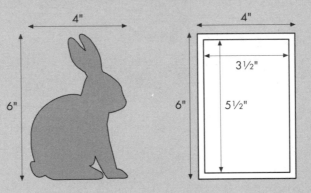

Step One: Multiply the number of pieces needed times the cut width (finished width plus total seam allowances) of the piece.

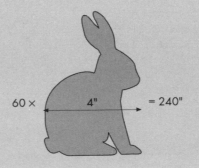

60 × 4" = 240"

Step Two: Divide the answer by the width of your fabric to determine how many rows your pieces will require. Most cotton fabric is approximately 44" wide. I use 40" as my fabric width to allow for fabric shrinkage, wide selvages, and just because it is an easier number to use. Round your answer up to the next whole number if necessary.

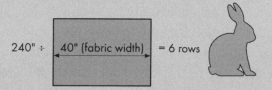

240" ÷ | 40" (fabric width) | = 6 rows

Step Three: Multiply the number of rows times the cut height (finished height plus seam allowances) of your piece. Your answer is 36" or 1 yard.

6 rows × | 6" | = 36" of fabric

Now you know that your 1 yard of fabric is sufficient. If you were going to purchase fabric for these rabbits, I would suggest 1¼ yards. One can never have too much fabric!

The average queen-size coverlet requires a total of approximately 12 yards of fabric. If you are putting together a group of fabrics to make a queen-size quilt, use this ballpark figure.

But What If I Run Out of Fabric?

OK, calm down and don't panic! This does happen, and when it does, you have two choices. You can either run around with a swatch of the fabric taped to your forehead, asking everyone you meet if they happen to have some, or you can come up with a creative solution. It's much easier to come up with a creative solution. Anyone can make the project as it was intended, but running out of fabric gives you the opportunity to contemplate alternatives.

Consider this dilemma as an opportunity for creativity. My experience tells me the creative solution is going to make your quilt unique and stand out from the rest. It is the creative solution that others notice and say, "What a neat idea!" Oh, by the way, don't announce to everyone that you ran out of fabric and had to make this change. Just let everyone think you are more creative than the average quilter! Just to prove my point, here are some run-out-of-fabric scenarios and creative solutions.

Problem: Your quilt has the same block with identical fabrics repeated throughout the quilt, and you run out of one of the fabrics used in the block.

Solution: Substitute a darker or lighter fabric in the same color. Depending upon how many blocks you'll need to contain this darker or lighter color, place them in a balanced way in the quilt. If the quilt has an odd number of blocks across, and one different block is necessary, place it in the center. If several blocks contain this darker version, they can be in the four corners. As long as you use this slightly different block(s) in a balanced way in the quilt, it will not look like you ran out of fabric. Your quilt will contain certain areas with more interest.

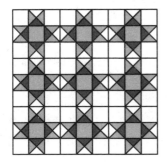

Original Quilt Plan

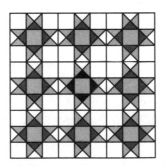

Solution 1

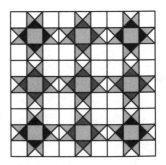

Solution 2

Problem: You intended to use a certain fabric for the border, but it's not long enough, and you'd rather not piece it.

Solution: Rather than letting everyone know you didn't have enough fabric, insert some sort of simple patchwork in the middle of each side between the two lengths. The inserted piece can be as simple as a triangle or square. Again, as long as you treat all the borders in the same way, it will look as if you intended a pieced section there. What if your fabric is long enough for the sides of the quilt, but not for the top and bottom once the sides are added? Add corner squares to the four corners of the quilt.

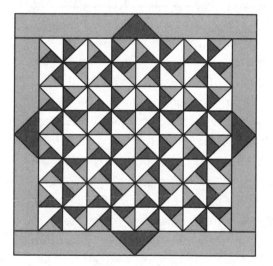

Triangles added

Corner squares added

Quiltmaking is a creative art, and patchwork offers plenty of opportunity to incorporate your creativity. Running out of fabric is just a gentle nudge to get your creative juices flowing.

Preparing Your Fabric (to wash or not to wash)

You may want to wash your fabric to preshrink it and to make sure darker fabrics will not bleed once they are used in patchwork with lighter fabrics. Fabrics in the red family in particular have a reputation for bleeding when you least desire it. Wash light and dark fabrics separately.

Orvus Paste is a good soap to use for washing your fabrics. It is available in most quilt shops in a little white jar marked "quilt soap." It is gentle to natural fibers, such as cotton, and rinses out easily. Orvus Paste is actually made for washing horses, so you may also find it at your local feed and grain store or tack shop. This product is concentrated so you need only 1 teaspoon to ¼ cup (depending on how soft your water is) per washing-machine load of warm water. Be sure to use warm water; it does not dissolve well in cold water.

Notice that I said you "may" want to wash your fabric, because there are really two schools of thought among quilters about whether to prewash fabric. Generally, those who hand piece and hand quilt prefer to wash their fabric before using it for the reasons stated above as well as to soften it for the hand-quilting process. However, many who machine piece and machine quilt prefer not to prewash. Some like the stiffer quality of the unwashed fabric during the machine-piecing process, while others want the slight bit of shrinkage to occur after the project is quilted so the fabric puffs slightly around the machine quilting.

If you prefer not to prewash, you should still test any suspect dark fabric that may bleed. To do this, hand wash swatches of your lightest fabrics and dark suspect fabrics together and let them dry on top of each other. If no color is transferred, you can probably safely use them in the same project. If a color transfer is evident, save the dark fabric for a project with dark fabrics.

I dry my fabric in the dryer, but I prefer to remove it from the dryer while it is still slightly damp and then iron it.

Use the square end of your ironing board rather than the pointed end to iron fabric. It goes much faster! To avoid distorting the fabric, move the iron between the cut ends rather than between the finished edges of the fabric (the selvages). There is less stretch in the length of the fabric.

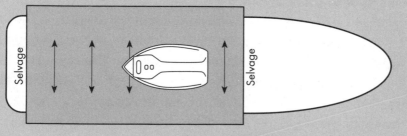

Iron along the length of the fabric.

Tools and Supplies

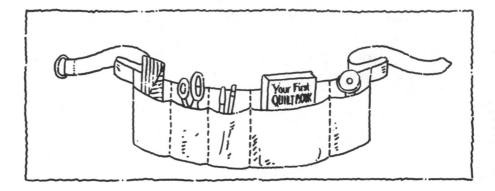

Many years ago, when my husband was in the market for woodworking tools, he declared that "one needs the right tools to do a good job." I take those words of wisdom to heart when it comes to my quiltmaking.

If you are fortunate, you will have a quilt shop within reasonable driving distance. Of course, reasonable driving distance to a quilter in search of a great quilt shop could be hours! Your local quilt shop is a wonderful source for supplies and classes to learn quiltmaking skills. If you do not have a quilt shop nearby, you can always let your fingers do the walking through free mail-order catalogs from the following:

Keepsake Quilting
Route 25B
PO Box 1618
Centre Harbor, NH 03226-1618
1-800-865-9458
Fax 1-603-253-8346
Foreign Orders: 1-603-253-8731

Clotilde, Inc.
B3000
Louisiana, MO 63353
1-800-772-2891
Fax 1-954 -493-8950
Foreign Orders: 1-954-491-2889

If you have ever walked into a quilt shop or browsed through a mail-order catalog of quilting supplies, you have seen an array of quilting products. You don't need to purchase one of everything, but using the right tool for the right job will not only make your quilting experience easier, it will yield a better product. The following list contains helpful tools and supplies.

Deciding What You'll Need (and deserve)

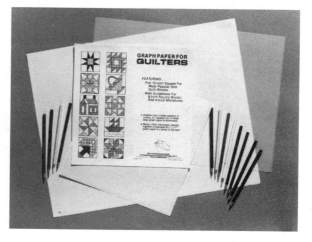

Graph Paper: Graph paper is used for creating and repoducing block designs. It makes no sense to use a blank piece of paper and attempt to draw accurately when ¼" graph paper is an option. Graph paper is available by the sheet or in a pad in a variety of sizes.

Colored Pencils: A box of colored pencils will come in handy to color patchwork designs so you can see what your color scheme will look like.

Template Plastic: Templates are used for cutting patchwork shapes. Templates for hand piecing are the finished size, while templates for machine piecing include a ¼"-wide seam allowance on all sides. They can be made of cardboard, but repetitive tracings eventually distort the corners and points. Clear plastic, sold in sheets, is a better choice for making accurate, durable templates.

Fabric-Marking Instruments: Sewing lines for hand-piecing templates and cutting lines for machine-piecing templates are marked on the wrong side of the fabric. Design lines for quilting are marked on the top of the quilt. Before marking the top of the quilt, always pretest any marking instrument on a scrap of the fabric you will be marking, to make sure you can easily remove the marks.

The following instruments are used for marking around templates on the *wrong* side of the fabric:

No. 2 Lead Pencil—Use on medium to dark fabrics and when sewing with medium to dark thread.

No. 4 Hard Lead Pencil—Use on light fabrics and when sewing with light-colored thread.

White Colored Pencil—Use on dark fabrics when you can't see a No. 2 lead pencil.

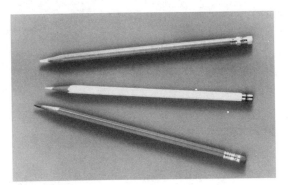

The following instruments are used for marking quilting designs on the *right* side of the fabric:

No. 4 Hard Lead Pencil—Use this lightly on light fabrics.

White Colored Pencil—Use on dark fabrics when you can't see a No. 4 hard lead pencil.

White or Gray Chalk Pencil—Use on dark fabrics when you can't see a white pencil.

Chalk and white colored pencils rub off easily, so wait until you are ready to quilt that area before you mark it.

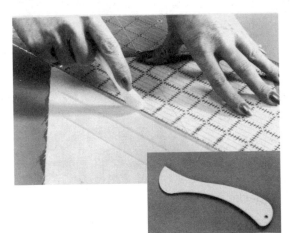

Hera Fabric Marker: This tool, commonly used in Japan to mark a crease on fabric, can be used to mark straight crease lines against a ruler on both light and dark solids and small-scale prints. The crease lines are more difficult to see on large-scale prints. You can mark before or after the quilt is sandwiched with batting. Use the curved spoon portion (not the point) of the marker against a ruler to make the crease! The crease remains until the fabric is washed.

Pins, Needles, and Related Things:

Use long, thin straight pins to join fabrics. It is more economical to purchase needles packaged in one size rather than a variety of sizes. Needles come in sizes by number. The larger the number, the smaller the needle. (I know, it's illogical.)

Sharps are used for hand piecing. I suggest you begin with a size 10.

Betweens are shorter than sharps and are used for hand quilting. I suggest you begin with a size 9 or 10.

Long darners are long, thin needles that are useful for hand basting. The long shank is comfortable to use when basting through several layers of fabric. I suggest a size 7.

Between   Sharp   Darner

Rustproof safety pins, 1" to 2" long, are used for pin basting the three layers together before machine quilting. To make this task easier on your fingers, you can use a grapefruit spoon or a Kwik Klip tool to close the pins after they are inserted in the fabric layers.

Pincushions are good, safe havens for your pin and needle supply. Magnetic pincushions are handy. A pin in the cushion is worth two in the couch!

Needle threaders can make the difference between threading a needle easily or total frustration. This inexpensive notion is definitely worth buying.

Thread and needle holders provide a secure place for your thread and needles while you are hand sewing or quilting. You only need to chase an elusive spool under a table once to understand the value of a thread holder.

Sewing and Quilting Threads: Use *medium-weight* sewing thread for hand piecing and machine piecing. Select an all-cotton or cotton-covered polyester thread in a color that blends with the color or value of your fabrics. If you are joining both dark and light patches, select a dark color. You can often rely on white, medium gray, and black threads since print fabrics camouflage the thread. When using solid fabrics, select thread to match.

Thread used for hand quilting is called *quilting thread* and is a little heavier weight than regular sewing thread. Some quilting threads have a stiffer quality. Personally, I prefer these stiffer threads because they are easier to guide through the eye of the needle. You can choose between all-cotton quilting thread or cotton-covered polyester quilting thread. Use the same type of quilting thread throughout the project.

Thread used for machine quilting can be either a *lightweight cotton thread* or a *monofilament nylon thread*. These can be used in both the needle and the bobbin. The monofilament nylon thread is available in clear for light-colored projects and smoke for dark-colored projects.

Quilting Hoops and Frames: The image of the little old lady leaning over the full-size floor frame is not a standard in today's quilting world. Some quilters do quilt at a full-size floor frame, but it is unnecessary even when making a full-size quilt. Quilting hoops are an alternative. They can be made of heavy wood (unlike thin embroidery hoops) and come in a variety of sizes. Some hoops are suspended on a floor stand or a lap stand. Select a hoop size that will secure the three layers of your project between the two hoops. Your underneath hand should be able to reach the middle of the hoop. An 18" or a 21" size is a good beginner size as long as your projects are larger than that.

Hand-held plastic frames are also available. They snap together for portability and come in a variety of square and rectangular sizes. These frames are particularly helpful when quilting the outside edge of a project because they snap onto the straight edges.

Thimbles: Thimbles are an accessory that you are either comfortable wearing when you sew or you aren't. For hand piecing, wearing a thimble is still a choice. When hand quilting, it is a different story. Your finger pushes the end of the needle through several layers, and before long, your finger screams for relief. To get accustomed to wearing a thimble, just wear it around the house for awhile. Later, when you use it to sew, it won't seem so awkward.

There are three types of thimbles: closed-top, open-top tailor's, and leather thimbles. The needle is pushed with the top of the closed-top thimble. The open-top tailor's thimble allows your nail to protrude from the top, and you use the side of the thimble to push the needle through. The tailor's thimble should fit snugly so your fingertip is roughly level with the open top. The leather thimble permits you to push from either the side or the top and is comfortable; however, it wears out quickly and needs to be replaced often. See how thimbles are used on pages 190–95.

Quilting Stencils: Stencils are plastic sheets with cutout designs. They are used to mark quilting patterns on the top of the quilt, either before or after layering with the backing and batting. Place the stencil on top of the quilt and mark through the slots with an appropriate marking tool. Stencils are available in a variety of sizes for both blocks and borders.

Sandpaper Tabs: These are little stick-on pieces of sandpaper that are placed on the underside of rotary rulers and templates. They help the rulers and templates grab the fabric and keep them from slipping. It is amazing how much stability these tabs offer. They are a handy notion.

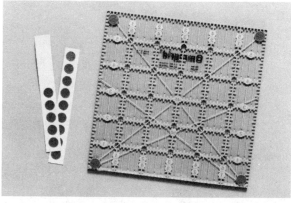

Sandpaper Marking Board: A fine piece of sandpaper adhered to a board is really helpful when marking around templates on the wrong side of the fabric. The sandpaper grabs the fabric so it won't move as you mark, giving you an accurate tracing.

You can easily make your own sandpaper surface by adhering a piece of fine-grade sandpaper to a file folder.

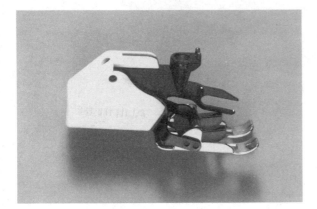

Walking Foot or Even-Feed Foot: This sewing-machine attachment helps feed the quilt layers into the needle at the same pace. It works in tandem with the feed dogs. The walking foot is particularly helpful when binding the quilt and when machine quilting straight lines or gentle curves.

Miscellaneous: Other things that will come in handy are ½"-wide masking tape, washable gluestick, and a fine-tip permanent pen.

Scissors: If you go to cut fabric with your scissors and the fabric folds instead of being cut, it is time to splurge on a new pair! You want to be able to cut accurate pieces easily. Most quilters use an inexpensive pair of scissors for cutting plastic template material and save a good pair of comfortable shears for cutting fabric. Small thread snips and a small pair of embroidery scissors also come in handy.

Using the Quilt-Essential Cutting Tools

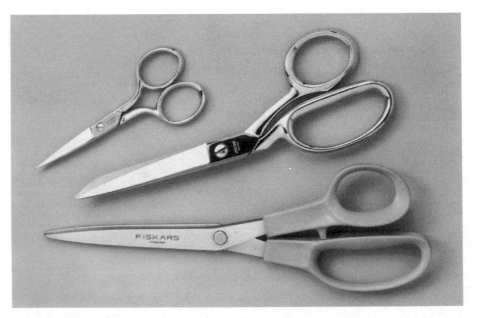

Seam Ripper: Since you just might make a mistake and need to take out a line of stitching, this little "unsewing" tool will certainly come in handy. Slip the long end of the ripper under every fourth or fifth stitch and cut. Pull the thread on the reverse side; it should come out easily.

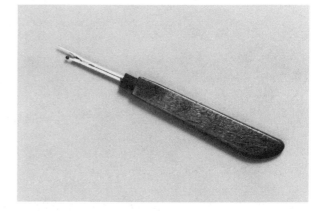

Rotary Cutter: If you are unfamiliar with this razorlike wheel that has become such a big part of quiltmaking in the last several years, let me caution you right up front. It is an extremely sharp instrument and should not be used carelessly. Some rotary cutters have guards that must be manually closed after each and every use. Other models have automatic guards. No matter what type of cutter you choose, use it with the utmost respect and keep it out of the reach of inquisitive children.

If you purchase a rotary cutter with a manual guard, make a special effort to close it each time you finish cutting, and it will soon become a habit.

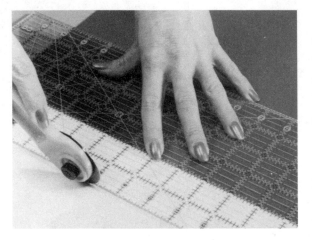

Several types and sizes of rotary cutters are available. Look at the options and choose the type most comfortable for you. Rotary cutters can cut through several layers of fabric; the larger the blade, the more layers you can cut. I suggest you begin with the medium-size cutter.

When you purchase your rotary cutter at a quilt shop, ask for a quick demonstration on its proper use. To rotary cut with the illustrated rotary cutter, wrap your hand around the handle, place your index finger on the ridged portion on top, and press down, following the edge of the ruler. Be sure the end of the handle is in your palm so your weight, not your wrist, presses down on the cutter. Place your other hand on top of the ruler, away from the cutting edge, and let at least one of your fingers extend to the other edge of the ruler to act as a backstop.

Avoid hitting pins with the blade. Running over pins will put nicks in the blade, and you will have to replace it. You will know that your blade has a nick if it misses cutting small bits of fabric.

If your blade does get a nick, and a replacement blade is not readily available, cut twice along the ruler edge. Chances are the uncut areas will not be repeated, and you can continue working until you can replace the blade.

Do not attempt to cut around lightweight plastic templates with your cutter. You will shave off bits of template and reduce the accuracy of your cuts.

Cutting Mat: Along with the cutter, you need a cutting mat. Trust me, you can't skip the mat! You will ruin your blade, not to mention the surface you cut on. Purchase the largest mat your sewing area can accommodate. You won't need to move your fabric as much with a large mat. Some mats have handy grid lines that help keep the fabric straight. Do not, however, use these lines to measure your fabric.

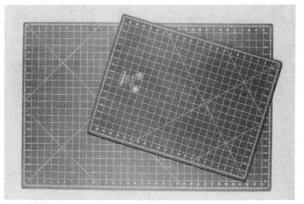

Rotary Rulers: There are a variety of heavy plastic rulers in different shapes and sizes you can use with the rotary cutter. They will not only save you lots of time, but will help you cut accurate pieces of fabric. In the beginning, 6" x 6", 6" x 12", 12½" x 12½", and 6" x 24" rulers are useful. You will probably want to add more rulers to your collection later.

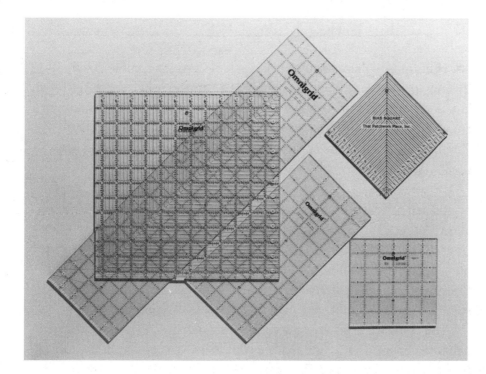

Pieced-Patchwork Block Designs

Hundreds of pieced patchwork block designs have come down through generations of quilters, and many more are being created today. You don't have to start from scratch and create your own block designs. However, if you want to try your hand at creating a new block, the simple grids that are the basis for most pieced patchwork blocks are a great place to start.

Simplifying the Grid System

Pieced patchwork designs are created by sewing together patches of fabric. Many traditional patchwork designs are based on standard grids. Understanding these grids enables you to reproduce patchwork blocks on paper so you can make templates for hand piecing, or to determine the size to cut each patch for machine patchwork. Knowing about the standard grids simplifies the patchwork process—trust me.

The standard grids are four patch, nine patch, five patch, and seven patch. To create a grid, you divide a square into a certain number of vertical and horizontal lines. To create the patchwork designs, you draw lines in the grid and shade the resulting units in different values. You do *not* have to use all the lines in the original grid in the patchwork design; they are simply the framework for the design.

Quilt blocks were traditionally given names. Sometimes, the block name was derived because the block was representational, such as the Pine Tree, Wedding Ring, and Spool blocks.

Name That Block!

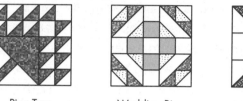

Pine Tree   Wedding Ring   Spool

Sometimes, it was a big stretch, like the Crow's Nest block. Does this look like a crow's nest to you?

Crow's Nest

Often, the name was in honor of something or someone, as in the Mississippi and Martha Washington Star blocks.

  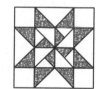

Mississippi   Martha Washington
                     Star

And sometimes, it's anybody's guess where the name came from. Mary in Maine and Tess in Texas may have created the same block, and each thought they had created an original patchwork design, so they each gave it a different name. For that reason, it is quite common for the same patchwork block to have several different names, and likewise, the same name given to totally different block designs. Talk about confusing!

This block is known as
Jacob's Ladder and
Road to California.

This block is
also known as
Road to California.

The good news is you don't have to know the names of different patchwork blocks. However, you will come to recognize familiar blocks by their names. Sometimes, you may see an unfamiliar block design and want to find out its name (a fairly common "quilter's query"). That is when a block dictionary comes in handy. A block dictionary has illustrations for many traditional blocks and the common names associated with each block. (See "Suggested Books" on page 221 for a list of block dictionaries.)

Likewise, when you create a patchwork block that is unlike any you have ever seen before, you'll want to check the block dictionary to see if it is indeed original. If you can't find it anywhere, feed it, love it, and give it a name.

Recognizing Traditional Block Grids

The block designs on pages 45–49 are based on traditional patchwork grids. For each block, such as Square within a Square, you'll see several illustrations. The first is the block design. In the second illustration, the grid on which the design is based has been placed on top of the design. Notice that the patches are filled with directional prints to indicate the suggested fabric grain. (To read more about fabric grain, see pages 57–59.) Finally, the sections of the block are "exploded" to show how it is assembled. Identical sections assembled in the same manner are shown joined.

Four Patch: A four-patch grid is based on a square that has been divided into 4, 16, or 64 equal units.

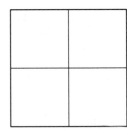
4 units

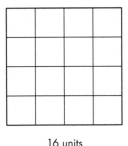
16 units

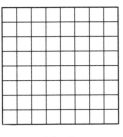
64 units

The following block designs are based on a 4-unit four patch:

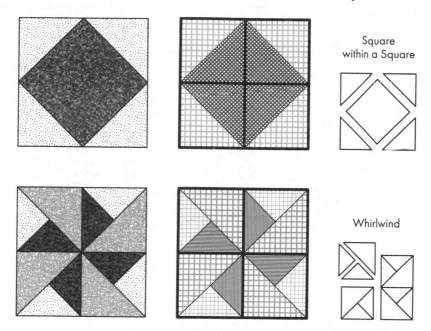

Square
within a Square

Whirlwind

Now take the 4-unit four patch one step further and divide each unit into four equal units. The result is a grid of 16 squares or a 16-unit four patch. The following block designs are based on a 16-unit four patch:

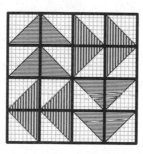

Dutchman's
Puzzle

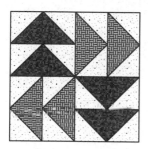
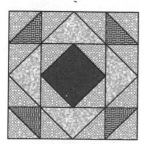
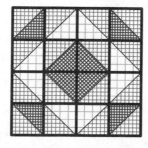
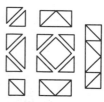

Magic Triangles

If you divide each unit into four equal units again, you get a 64-unit four patch. This means you can have lots of little pieces to sew together to make your block design. The important word is *can*. I would suggest that you hold off jumping into blocks with a large number of pieces for awhile. The following block designs are based on a 64-unit four patch:

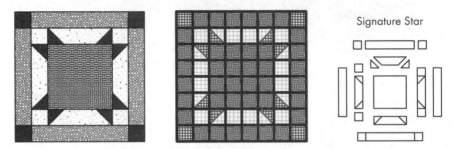

Signature Star

I just made this one up to show that not all the patches have to be small!

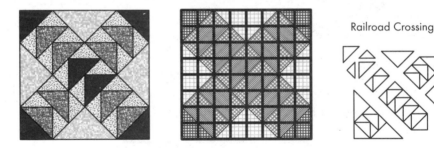

Railroad Crossing

Nine Patch: Now that we've strolled through some four-patch designs, let's take a look at a different grid. The nine-patch grid is a square that has been divided into 9 or 36 equal units. I think you will like the nine-patch grid because it allows you to produce blocks with lots of variety.

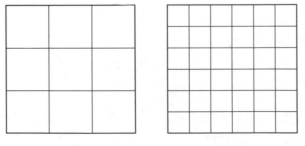

9 units   36 units

The following block designs are based on a 9-unit nine patch:

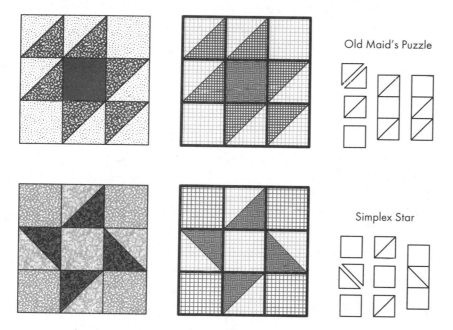

Old Maid's Puzzle

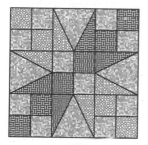

Simplex Star

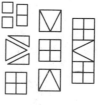

The following block designs are based on a 36-unit nine patch:

Bird of Paradise

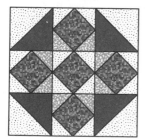

Sawtooth
Patchwork

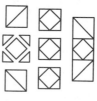

Five Patch: I know it appears the five patch is out of sequence here—we went from the four patch to the nine patch and then to the five patch. But actually, we are following the number of divisions in the block. A four patch has 2 sections along the sides of the block, a nine patch has 3, and a five patch has 5.

The following block designs are based on a five patch:

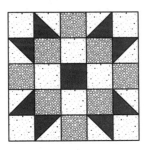

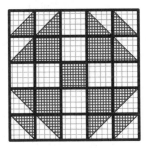

Five Patch Star

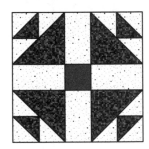

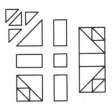

Wild Goose Chase

Seven Patch: A seven patch is divided into 7 sections along the sides for a total of 49 units.

The following block designs are based on a seven patch. I designed these myself and gave them names.

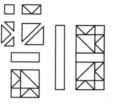

Ursula's Favorite

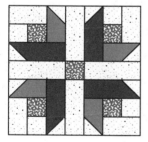

Carol's Favorite

Creating and Reproducing Block Designs

One reason to know about traditional block grids is because they provide a blank format for creating your own patchwork designs. Simply connect points on the grid to create shapes, and shade in different values to create a patchwork design.

Another reason to know about traditional grids is because they are the key to reproducing patchwork blocks. Once you determine the grid for a design, you can reproduce the block and create the necessary templates to make the block, or determine the cut size of simple shapes for machine patchwork. For instance, suppose you saw the following quilt at a quilt show and you would love to make it. Look for a block unit that appears to repeat itself throughout the quilt and isolate the block.

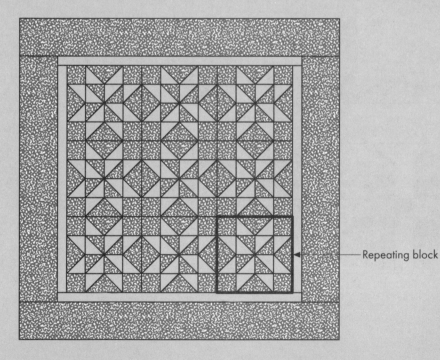

Repeating block

Isolate a square or square unit in the block. Then note how the square or square unit is repeated in the patchwork. Soon you'll see a grid emerging. This block is based on a four-patch grid with four divisions along the top, bottom, and sides.

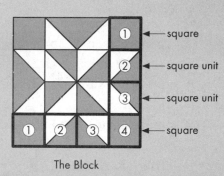

The Block

Draw the block size you want to make and divide it into a four-patch grid. For this example, let's make the above design in an 8" block. Draw the 8" block on graph paper with a pencil and ruler to make sure your lines are accurate. Divide the 8" block into a four-patch grid (8" ÷ 4 = 2"). You should have sixteen 2" squares. Draw the diagonal lines as shown and watch the design emerge. Shade the sections of the design to match the values you saw in the quilt at the quilt show. You have just reproduced the block design! Give yourself a pat on the back.

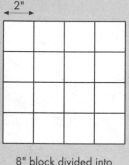

8" block divided into a four-patch grid

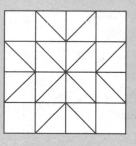

Add diagonal lines.

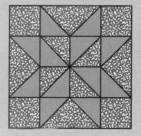

Shade in values.

Now you can see the value of understanding the basic patchwork grids. But wait, that one was simple. After all, the 8" block was easily divided into a four-patch grid. What if you wanted to make that same four-patch grid into a 9" block? You would need to divide the 9" block into four units (9" ÷ 4 = 2¼"). OK, it took a little math, but that wasn't bad. But what if you wanted to make a 9-unit nine patch into an 8" block? That would be 8" divided by 3. This one is not quite so simple mathematically. However, there is a simple way to create any block size in any grid.

Continued on page 52

Draw Any Block Size (you'll love this trick!)

You can make any block design in any size. I'm taking this process one step at a time so you can see how easy it is. This is a valuable tool because it offers great flexibility in your patchwork.

Example: Divide an 8" block into a 9-unit nine patch:

Step One: Draw the desired-size block on graph paper (8").

Step Two: Go to the next highest number (above the block size) that you can divide equally by the number of divisions you want to make. In our case, we want to divide the block into thirds (three sections a side). The next highest number above 8 that you can divide equally by 3 is 9. Find 9 on your ruler and divide by 3 ($9 \div 3 = 3$). Place a chalk mark at the 3", 6", and 9" lines on the ruler. The chalk marks provide a visual reference so you don't need to remember the numbers on the ruler.

Step Three: Place the 0 mark on the ruler at the lower left corner of the block and slide the right side of the ruler until the 9" mark hits the right side. Mark the 3" and 6" locations on the paper with a dot.

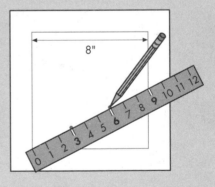

Step Four: Draw a vertical line through each dot you just made. You have divided the block vertically into thirds!

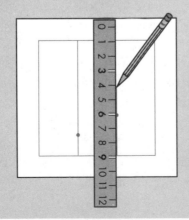

Step Five: Move the 0 mark on the ruler to the top left corner and slide the ruler until the 9" mark is on the bottom of the block. Mark the 3" and 6" locations on the paper with a dot.

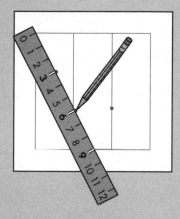

Step Six: Draw a horizontal line through each dot. You now have an 8" block divided into a nine patch!

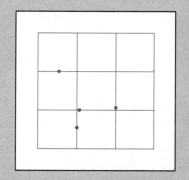

8" block divided into a nine-patch grid

By the way, if you want to divide an 8" block into a 36-unit nine patch (6 units on each side), go to the next number above 8 you can divide equally by 6. The answer is 12. Find 12 on your ruler and divide it by 6 (12 ÷ 6 = 2). Mark every 2" on the ruler and continue as before.

But what if you wanted to make a 12" five patch? Go to the next highest number above 12 that you can divide equally by 5. The answer is 15. Go to 15 on the ruler and divide it by 5 (15 ÷ 5 = 3). Mark every 3" on the ruler and continue as before.

Continued on page 54

OK, one more. What if you want to divide a 12" block into a seven patch? What is the next highest number above 12 that you can divide by 7? The answer is _____. Of course—14. Go to 14 on the ruler and divide by 7 (14 ÷ 7 = 2). Mark every 2" on the ruler and continue as before.

What happens if the end number on the ruler goes right off the square when it is placed diagonally? This can happen if the block size you are making is small and the grid size large. For instance, if you are making an 8" block into a seven patch, the next number above 8 that divides equally by 7 is 14. When you place the ruler diagonally on the block so the 14" mark hits the right side, it goes right off the block! But there is a solution. Extend the right-side line as long as you need to, to place the 14" mark on that line. Mark the dots as before, even if they fall outside your block. Mark the dividing lines as before. When you mark the dots in the opposite direction, extend the bottom line.

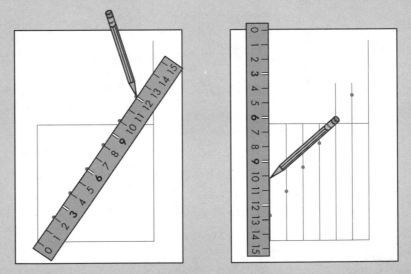

To make an 8" block into a seven patch, extend the block line.

Draw vertical lines.

I can't urge you enough to practice this neat trick. It will let you create the blocks you want in any size. Freedom can be a wonderful feeling!

Pieced-Patchwork Techniques

Before you proceed, consider whether you will sew your patches together by hand or by machine. The process you use to make the same patchwork block from this point onward will differ, depending on your sewing choice.

Stitching: By Hand or Machine?

No "tug-of-war" really exists between those who prefer handwork and those who prefer machine work. It simply comes down to your favorite method of working or the preferred method for the project at hand. It is perfectly acceptable to use both in the same project. You may decide to hand piece your blocks, then assemble them and add the borders by machine. You may choose to piece by machine and hand quilt your project.

If you exhibit tendencies for handwork, the sewing machine might make you tense as you work on your first project. If you are comfortable using a machine, and handwork seems like an exercise in how our ancestors created patchwork, it might feel uncomfortably slow. Once you feel comfortable with either method, I suggest you at least try the alternate method, if for no other reason than for the experience. The following questions for beginning quilters will give you some insight into your preferences.

Take the Preference Test

Answer "yes" or "no" to the following questions.

☐ 1. Do you own a sewing basket?

☐ 2. Is your sewing machine stored in someone else's garage or another remote location?

☐ 3. Do you like to sit and visit with friends and family, but still keep busy doing something else?

☐ 4. Are you on the run with children to dentist appointments, etc., and a fan during their sporting events?

☐ 5. Do you feel relaxed when you hold a sewing needle in your hand?

☐ 6. Do you enjoy the sense of creating a little bit at a time?

☐ 7. Do you like to take new experiences at a slower pace?

☐ 8. Do you enjoy working with your hands?

☐ 9. Does your breathing rate increase when you sit at a sewing machine?

☐ 10. Do you consider sewing at the machine "work"?

If you answered "yes" to most of these questions, hand piece your first patchwork project. If you answered "no" to most of these questions, answer the following questions.

☐ 1. Do you own a sewing machine?

☐ 2. Do you know where it is?

☐ 3. Have you ever sewn on a sewing machine?

☐ 4. Do you clean the lint from the bobbin area regularly?

☐ 5. Do you change the needle regularly?

☐ 6. Do you breathe at relaxed intervals when machine sewing?

☐ 7. It's 11 p.m.—do you know where your owner's manual is?

☐ 8. Do you know what the buttons and knobs on your machine do?

☐ 9. Do you "escape" to sew at the machine?

☐ 10. Can you get your machine up and running in less than 15 minutes?

If you answered "yes" to most of these questions, machine piece your first patchwork project.

Your Official Pep Talk

Most quilters look back at their first quilt project with a smile and a few chuckles. Your first steps may be a bit awkward. However, with each and every project you make, you will feel more comfortable and you will gain understanding and skill.

I also want to stress the importance of accuracy in patchwork, whether you sew by hand or machine. Ballpark measurements in cutting and sewing don't work in patchwork. I tell my beginning quilters that

⅟₁₆ of an inch really *does* matter. A project that calls for 16 squares across will be 1" off if the squares are as much as ⅟₁₆" too large or too small.

I don't say this to scare you, but to stress the importance of accuracy in making templates and in marking, cutting, and sewing the pieces. Accuracy is worth the effort because it makes the assembly process easier and more fun.

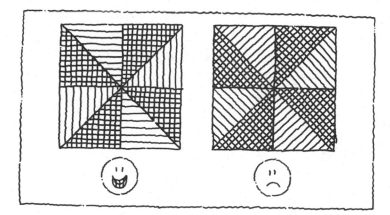

Knowing the Fabric Grain: It Can Make or Break You!

Before we mark and cut fabric pieces, we need to talk about fabric grain. Fabric has three grains.

The *lengthwise grain* runs parallel with the selvages and has very little stretch. If you tug on the length of the fabric, you will hear it snap.

The *crosswise grain* runs perpendicular to the selvages and has a slight amount of stretch. If you tug on the width of the fabric, you will see slight rolls and it will make a lower-pitch sound than the lengthwise grain. Both the lengthwise and crosswise grains of the fabric are considered the straight of grain.

The *diagonal grain* that runs at a 45° angle with the straight of grain is called the true bias. True bias has the greatest amount of stretch, and if you tug against the bias, you won't hear a thing!

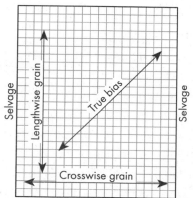

Now you are probably asking, "Why do I need to know this?" Because normally, you'll want the straight grain on your patchwork pieces to run vertically and horizontally in the block. A checked pattern is used to illustrate the horizontal and vertical straight grain in the Sawtooth Star block on the left below. You definitely do not want those stretchy bias edges on the outside edges of the block. If you are going to rotary cut your fabric pieces for machine piecing, rotary cut them so the grain will be vertical and horizontal once you place the pieces in the patchwork block. Mark a straight-grain arrow on any templates you use for hand or machine piecing to coincide with the direction of the straight grain in the block as shown in the second part of the illustration.

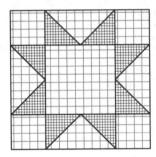 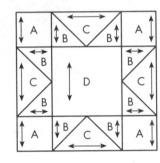 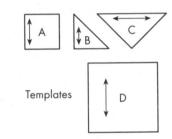

Templates

The third part of the illustration (above) shows the hand-piecing template shapes required for this block and the direction of the straight-grain arrow on each template. You will notice that there are two different-size triangles (B and C). The direction of the straight-grain arrow in B is on the short side of the triangle, and the direction of the straight-grain arrow in C is on the long side of the triangle. When the straight grain is on the short sides of the triangle, it is called a half-square triangle. When the straight grain is on the long side of the triangle, it is called a quarter-square triangle.

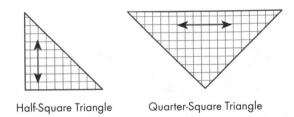

Half-Square Triangle   Quarter-Square Triangle

Look at the second part of each block design on pages 45–49. Directional fabrics are used to suggest the correct fabric grain. Note how the fabric grain falls in these blocks, and you will soon become accustomed to how fabric grain is typically used in patchwork.

There's Always an Exception!

The exception to the rule is that fabric grain can vary for design purposes or for ease of cutting, when the fabric pieces are *not used at the outside edge of the block*. For example, in the first block below, a striped fabric is used for template B. To achieve the desired visual effect, the long side of the template is placed on the straight grain of the fabric so the bias edges are along the vertical and horizontal seam lines inside the patchwork block. The key word here is *inside*, where the edges will be secured to straight-grain edges of the adjoining pieces. In the second block, a square cut on the straight grain is placed on-point inside the block. In this instance, the bias grain in the middle of the square is secured by the half-square triangles that surround it.

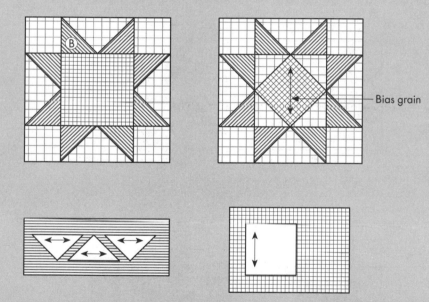

Bias grain

Following a Piecing Sequence

When sewing patches together, the goal is to sew straight seams in a logical fashion. The diagrams illustrating the logical order is called a piecing sequence. (A piecing sequence is provided for each block at the beginning of the projects in this book.) Sometimes combining units to create square sections of the original grid is easiest. Other times, you will join center sections and add corner units. Review each block and follow the piecing sequence to become familiar with routine combinations used to create blocks.

If you are hand piecing, you may sew patches that have "set-in" pieces, since these are not difficult to do by hand (see page 72). If you machine piece the block, however, you may want to avoid these set-in pieces in the beginning, since they can be tricky. The following example shows how a block design can be sewn *with* set-in pieces or *without* set-in pieces, simply by altering the seam lines and piecing sequence.

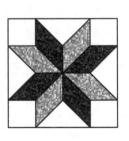

The corners and side triangles will be set-in pieces.

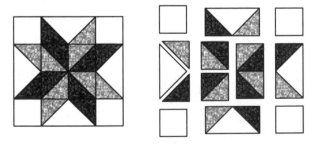

This block has no set-in pieces.

Piecing by Hand: The Game Plan

If you have decided to hand piece your first project, the following information is provided with each project in this book.

- The number of different fabrics and how much of each one is needed.
- A drawing of each different finished-size pattern shape so you can make templates. These template shapes have identification letters and fabric grain-line arrows.
- How many pieces to mark and cut from each fabric. This is your cutting list.
- How to sew the fabric pieces together in a logical sequence. This is your piecing sequence.

Gather your fabrics, make the necessary templates, mark the shapes on the wrong side of the fabrics, and cut them out ¼" from the pencil line. Remember, you are adding the ¼"-wide seam allowance to your fabric patches as you cut them out.

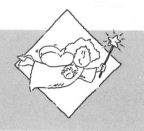

Raise your right hand and repeat after me, "I promise not to cut out these shapes on the drawn lines. I will remember to cut ¼" away from the lines I have drawn."

Lay out the patches like puzzle pieces to form the block design. Pin the patches together and hand sew with a running stitch to make small units. Join the small units to make the block. The following steps for hand piecing will take you from templates to patchwork block.

Step One: Make finished-size templates. Using removable tape, secure a piece of plastic template material to each template page in the project. Trace the template shapes onto the plastic, using a ruler and pencil or a fine-tip permanent marker. Mark the identification letter and straight-grain arrow on the templates. The marked side will be the right side of the template. Cut out on the inside edge of the line. Confirm the accuracy of your template by placing it back on the drawing; you should be able to just see the printed line along the edge. If not, make necessary corrections to your template. Remember, the seam allowance will be added when the fabric pieces are cut. (Am I beginning to sound paranoid about remembering to add the seam allowance?)

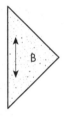

Step Two: Following the project cutting list, mark the fabric: Place the wrong side of the template (the unmarked side) face up on the wrong side of the fabric (straight-grain arrow coincides with the straight grain of the fabric). Use a pencil and mark around the outside edge of the template. See "Fabric-Marking Instruments" on page 33 for marking options. Hold the pencil at a 45° angle and mark the lengthwise grain first, then the crosswise grain, and finally the bias. Instead of marking around the corners, mark straight lines that will intersect at the corners. As you move the template over to mark the next piece, be sure to leave at least ½" between the pieces so you will have enough fabric for both ¼"-wide seam allowances. Mark the shapes in a row when you can; they will be easier to cut out.

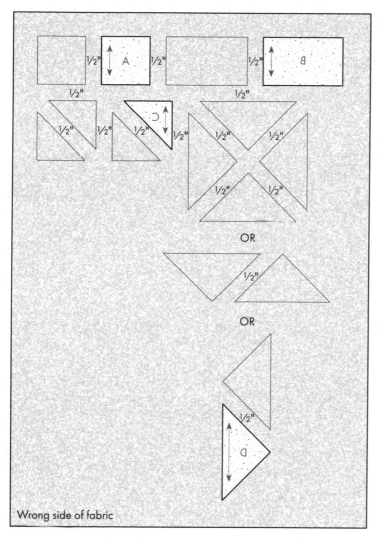

Wrong side of fabric

Place wrong side of templates face up.

Before marking around the templates, adhere sandpaper tabs to the plastic templates and place the fabric on a sandpaper board to keep the fabric and templates from moving; your pieces will be more accurate. See "Sandpaper Marking Board" on page 37.

Step Three: Cut the pieces ¼" from the drawn lines on all sides to allow for seam allowances. Use a pair of scissors and estimate the ¼"-wide seam allowance, or place the ¼" mark of the rotary ruler on the line and rotary cut the pieces, adding the seam allowances as you cut. Personally, I think the latter is the easiest approach to this task.

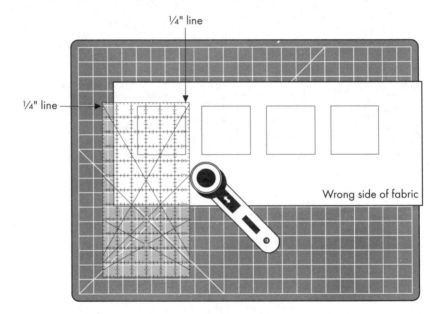

As you cut the fabric pieces, pin them right side up on a piece of scrap fabric or flannel to create the patchwork pattern as if you were assembling a puzzle. Placing the pieces in the correct position will make sewing the block together more efficient.

To make a simple portable patchwork carrier for your blocks, cut a piece of fabric, 18" x 40". Place two 16" x 16" squares of flannel on top of each other, at the right side of the fabric piece as shown. Fold the outer fabric in half and stitch down the middle, catching one edge of the flannel squares. Place the fabric patches for two blocks on the flannel so they are ready to pick up and hand piece.

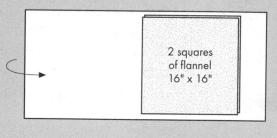

2 squares
of flannel
16" x 16"

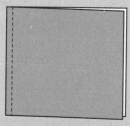

Fold and stitch the middle,
catching the flannel squares.

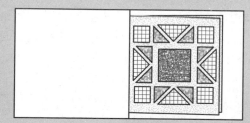

Step Four: Following the piecing sequence, pick up the first two patches to be joined and place them right sides together. Place a straight pin from front to back at the beginning of the seam line and back

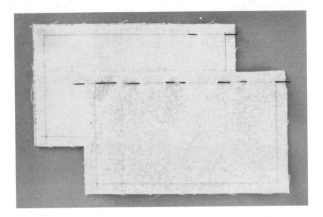

through to the front. I usually select the fabric where it is easiest to see the pencil line as the front piece. Turn the patches over and place a straight pin in the same way at the end of the seam line. If more pins are necessary, continue to add them through the seam lines from the back. The top piece in the photo shows the two pieces from the front with the first pin. The lower piece shows how the two pieces look from the back with the remaining pins.

Step Five: Sew the patches together. Use a size 10 Sharp needle. Thread the needle with a single strand of thread (about 15" long) that will blend with your fabrics. Do not knot the end of the thread.

For stress-free needle threading, try the following tips.

- To make the eye of the needle more visible, hold it over a plain white surface.
- If you can't thread the eye in one direction, turn the needle around and try it from the other direction. It is easier to thread the needle in the direction it was milled.
- Cut the end of the thread at an angle.
- If all else fails, grab a good needle threader and use it. They make these things so we don't become frustrated!

a. With the beginning pin still in place, insert the needle on the sewing line and pull the thread, leaving a tail about ¼" long. Remove the first pin. Take two stitches in the same place. This is called a backstitch and it will secure the end of the thread. In the following photos, black thread is used for illustration purposes.

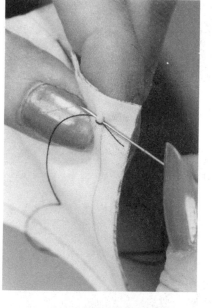

b. Holding the fabric taut with your left hand (or right if left-handed), begin to weave the fabric onto the needle, gathering the fabric from behind the needle with your index finger until you have several stitches on the needle. The first photo (top) shows how the fabric is being woven onto the needle from the front. The second photo (bottom) shows how gathered stitches appear on the back.

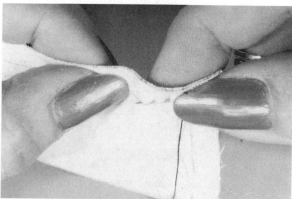

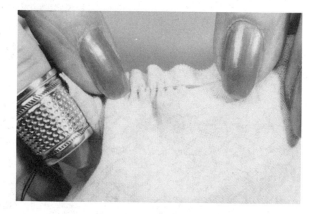

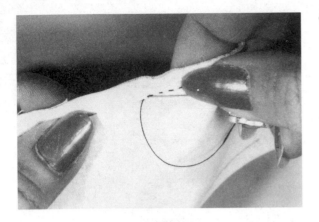

c. Pull the needle and thread through the fabric, relaxing the gathers, and insert it behind the thread to begin again. Putting the needle behind the exiting thread will create a backstitch that locks the stitches in place.

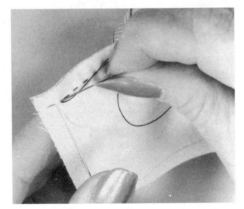

d. Continue along the pencil line, backing out the pins from behind the patches as you approach them. When you come to the end pin, back out the point, but keep the head intact until you backstitch (take two stitches in the same spot) at the end. Cut the thread, leaving a ¼" tail. In the photo at left, notice how the pin at the end is still in place until the needle is inserted.

Instead of ending with a backstitch, you can end with this neat little knot, called a lingerie knot.

1. Take one backstitch at the end.
2. Insert the needle in again as if you are going to backstitch, but leave it in the fabric.

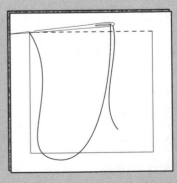

3. Take the two threads from the eye and place them under the point of the needle in the direction of the single thread.

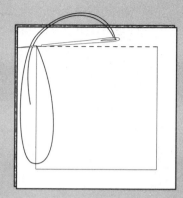

4. Take the single thread and place it under the point of the needle to the opposite side.

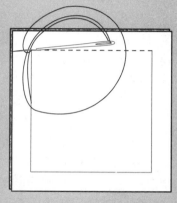

5. Pull the needle and thread through the fabric to make the knot. Cut the thread.

To remember how to make the lingerie knot, the following knot tall tale may help. *Two buddies went to visit their friend* (the two threads from the eye under the point of the needle). *Their friend was feeling a bit antisocial and left* (the single thread under the point to the other side).

Step Six: Open the joined patches, move the two seam allowances to the darker side of the patch, and finger-press (move your fingers along the seam line to crease it). While this may not seem important, it will make joining subsequent pieces easier. Place the patches in the correct block location and pick up the next two patches to be joined.

Join Seamed Patches (yea, they match!)

When it is time to join two seamed patches (or patchwork rows or sections), match the intersecting seams. Pick up the two units you are joining and pin the ends as if you were joining two single patches (see Step Four on page 66). Place a pin vertically through the seams to be matched, moving the seam allowances in opposite directions. If more pins are needed, add them from the back horizontally along the seam lines.

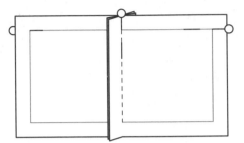

Place seams in opposite directions.

Sew the seam line as usual, but as you approach the seam intersection, take a backstitch on one side of the seam. Slide the needle through the seam allowances, pull the thread tight, and take a backstitch on the other side of the seam allow-

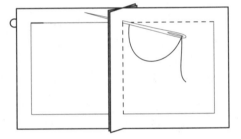

ances. *Do not sew the seam allowances down*. Continue stitching to the end of the seam line. Finger-press the seams toward the darker fabric.

Hand Piecing on Your Own

The hand-piecing information presented so far is enough to get you through the beginner projects in this book. The following information will help you when you are ready to go on and hand piece patchwork on your own.

- If you are using your own patchwork design, draw it on graph paper in the desired size. Determine the necessary templates (one for each shape and size piece). Identify each template with a letter and draw the fabric grain line on the template. Follow the procedure for making finished-size templates as described in Step One on page 62.
- If you go to the grocery store with a shopping list in hand, you are more likely to arrive home with the items you intended to purchase.

If you make a cutting list of how many pieces to mark and cut from each fabric, you will also be more efficient. Below is the cutting list for one Simplex Star block.

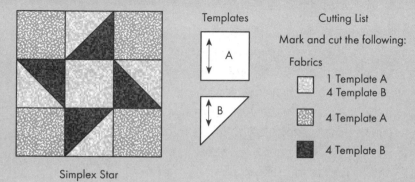

Simplex Star

However, if you were going to make a quilt that has 25 of these blocks, you'd simply multiply the number of pieces listed for each template times 25 to find the number of pieces to cut for the entire quilt.

- Many block designs require cutting a reverse piece. This is often done when a patchwork shape is asymmetrical. If you turn a square over, it is the same shape on both sides; it is symmetrical. Triangle C, shown below, is an example of an asymmetrical shape. When you turn it over, you get the reverse of the original shape. Directions for cutting reverse pieces are indicated by the letter "r" following the identifying template letter (such as template Cr). You don't need to make a separate template for reverse pieces. To mark reverse pieces, place the template *right side up* on the wrong side of the fabric. Remember, the right side of the template is the side with identification marks on it.

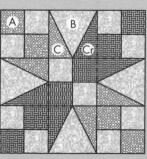

Bird of Paradise

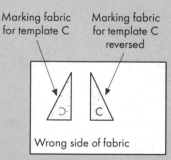

Wrong side of fabric

Continued on page 72

- When you stitch a piece into a corner, it is called a set-in piece; this is not as difficult as you might think. It is generally done in two steps. When you hand piece, you can sew set-in pieces with relative ease. In the first example, the corner squares and side triangles are set in. In the second example, the added seam lines, indicated by the dotted lines, allow you to piece the block with all straight seams; no set-in seams are needed. This option is available when you prefer not to sew set-in pieces (see page 60).

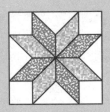

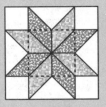

This block requires set-in pieces.

The added seams in this block eliminate the set-in pieces.

To sew a set-in piece by hand, pin one side as you would normally pin a straight seam and sew to the end pin. Slip the needle through the seam allowances. Pivot the fabric, pin the remaining side of the seam, sew to the end, and backstitch.

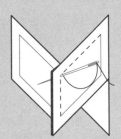

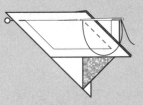

Slip the needle through the seam allowances.

Pivot, pin, and sew the remaining seam.

If you are sewing a set-in piece to one piece of unseamed fabric rather than two seamed pieces, clip the seam allowance at the V and proceed as described above.

Cut here.

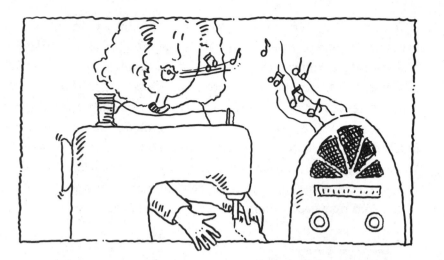

If you have decided to machine piece your first project, the following information is provided with each project in this book.

- The number of different fabrics and how much of each one is needed for the project.
- How many and what size pieces to cut from each fabric, using a rotary cutter and ruler. The cut pieces include ¼"-wide seam allowances on all sides. This is your cutting list.
- What templates to make if machine-piecing templates are necessary. Machine-piecing templates include the ¼"-wide seam allowance on all sides. Mark the *cutting line* for the templates on the wrong side of the fabric and cut these out on the cutting line. Sometimes you can cut the pieces with the template attached to the ruler (see pages 81–82).
- How to make strip-pieced units if the patchwork is created by strip piecing. Directions include how many and what size strip(s) to cut from each fabric, how to sew the strips together, and how to crosscut them.
- How to sew the fabric pieces together in a logical sequence. This is your piecing sequence.

Gather your fabrics, make any necessary machine-piecing templates, and rotary cut your fabric pieces. Remember, the ¼"-wide seam allowances (½" total) are already included in the size of the pieces. Lay the pieces out like puzzle pieces to form the block design. Follow the piecing sequence to machine sew the units together. If the block is strip-pieced, follow the instructions to cut and sew together the strips.

Rotary Cut: It's Magic

Your rotary cutter and rotary rulers will permit you to cut simple shapes one by one or several at a time by layering the fabric—you'll think it's magic. You can easily cut strips, rectangles, squares, half-square triangles, and quarter-square triangles as long as the measurement can be located on the ruler, thus eliminating the need for making templates for most of the pieces. *Measurements for all pieces include the standard ¼"-wide seam allowance on all sides.*

1. Before you begin to rotary cut strips from your fabric, you'll need to make a clean-cut edge. Fold the fabric in half with selvages matching. You may need to raise one edge of the fabric in order to align the selvages.

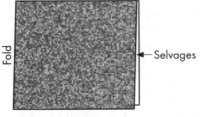

The fabric is even at the top, but the selvages are not parallel.

The selvages are parallel, and the uneven top is ready to be "clean cut."

2. Place the fabric on the cutting mat with the fold closest to you and the uneven edges to your left. (If you are left-handed, place the uneven edges to your right.) If you prefer, you can bring the bottom fold up to meet the selvages for a shorter cutting distance.

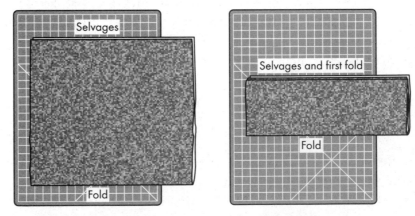

Fabric folded once

Fabric folded twice

3. Place a 6" x 6" square ruler on the bottom fold near the edge to be cut, making sure it is straight. Butt a 6" x 24" (or 6" x 12" ruler for double-folded fabric) ruler against the square so the edge of the long ruler just covers the uneven edge of the fabric. Remove the square and make a clean cut along the edge of the ruler. Roll the rotary cutter away from you, using firm, downward pressure. Be careful not to let the ruler slip out of position as you cut. Create a backstop against the outside edge of the ruler with your little finger. See page 40 for detailed rotary-cutting instructions.

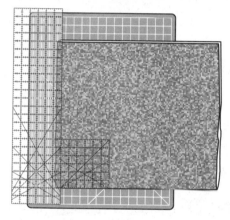
Align rulers.

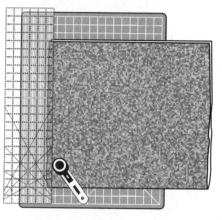
Make clean cut.

Right-handed

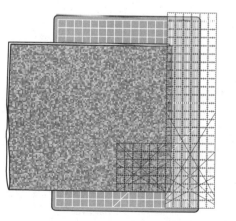
Align rulers.

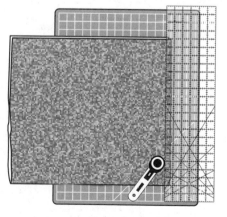
Make clean cut.

Left-handed

4. To cut strips, align the clean-cut edge of the fabric with the desired ruler marking, and a horizontal line on the ruler with the fold.

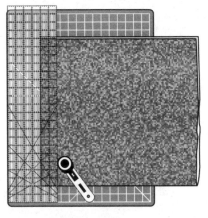

Right-handed

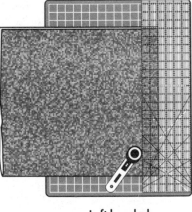

Left-handed

After you have cut the required number of strips, pin the clean-cut edges of the remaining fabric together before putting it aside. That way, the fabric will be ready if you need to cut more strips later. Simply remove the pins and cut.

To cut squares and rectangles, place the folded strip horizontally on your cutting mat.

Cutting Multiple Squares and Rectangles

1. Remove the selvages from the strip. To do this, place a horizontal line of a ruler along the cut edges of the strip near the selvages. Butt a second ruler next to the first ruler. Remove the first ruler and cut along the edge of the second ruler.

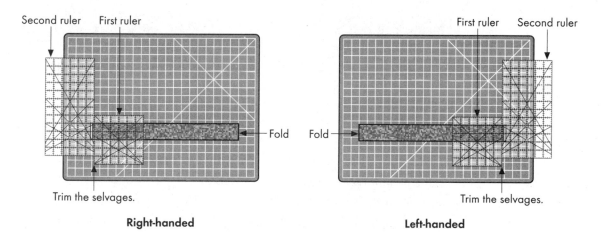

Right-handed   **Left-handed**

2. Align the required measurement on the ruler with the newly cut edge of the strip. Cut along the edge of the ruler. Continue along the strip until you have cut the required number of squares or rectangles. The diagram below illustrates how to cut 2" squares.

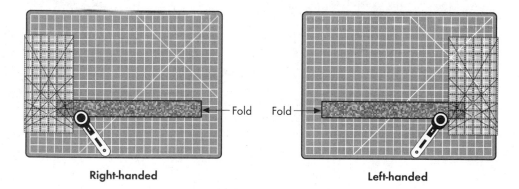

Right-handed   **Left-handed**

The diagram below illustrates how to cut 2" x 4" rectangles. If the strip is 2" wide, align the 4" mark on the ruler with the cut edge.

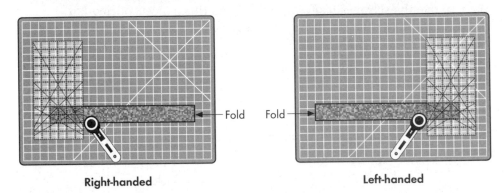

Right-handed   **Left-handed**

Cutting a Small Number of Squares and Rectangles

But what if you only need a few squares or rectangles? There is no need to cut an entire strip of fabric. With your fabric folded in half, simply cut a strip long enough to accommodate the number of squares or rectangles you need. For example, let's say you only need four 2" x 6" rectangles. Trim the selvages and cut a strip 2" x 12" as shown. Turn the layered strips, align the 2" and 6" marks on the ruler with the cut edges, and cut. You now have four rectangles. Remember, you are cutting two at a time from the layered fabric.

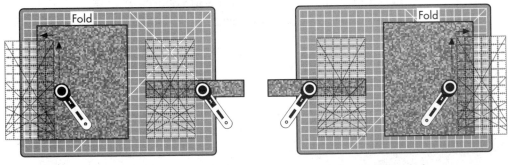

Right-handed   **Left-handed**

If you need only one square or rectangle, cut pieces from a single layer of fabric. Align the required measurement on the ruler with the clean-cut edges of the fabric. The diagrams below illustrate how to cut one square. When cutting a rectangle, align the two different measurements on the ruler with the cut edges of the fabric.

Cutting Only One Square or Rectangle

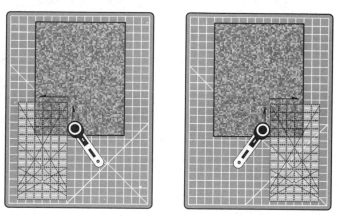

Cut a single square from a single layer.

Right-handed   **Left-handed**

Half-square and quarter-square triangles are exactly the same shape. The only difference between them is the direction of the fabric grain.

Cutting Half-Square and Quarter-Square Triangles

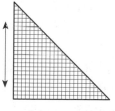 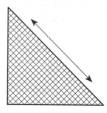

Half-Square Triangle   Quarter-Square Triangle

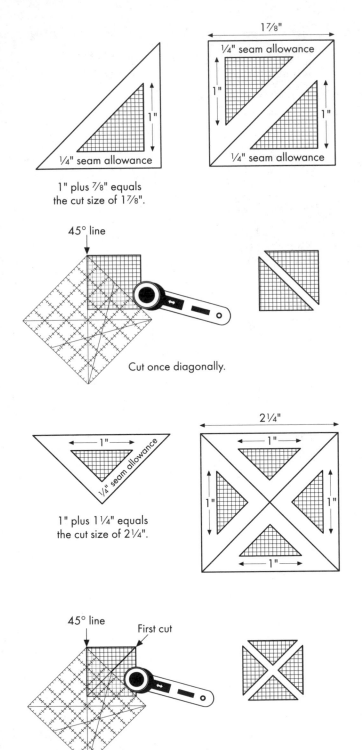

1" plus ⅞" equals
the cut size of 1⅞".

45° line

Cut once diagonally.

1" plus 1¼" equals
the cut size of 2¼".

45° line

First cut

Cut twice diagonally.

To cut two half-square triangles (with the straight grain on the short sides of the triangle), *cut a square ⅞" larger than the finished short side of the triangle* you need. Align the 45° line on your ruler with the straight edge of the square. Cut the square once diagonally from corner to corner.

To cut multiple triangles, determine how many squares you need to cut. Since 1 square yields 2 half-square triangles, divide the number of triangles you need by 2. For example, if you need 20 triangles, cut 10 squares once diagonally.

To cut four quarter-square triangles (straight grain on the long side of the triangle), *cut a square 1¼" larger than the finished long side of the triangle* you need. Cut the square twice diagonally.

To cut multiple quarter-square triangles, first determine how many squares you need to cut. Since 1 square yields 4 quarter-square triangles, divide the number of triangles you need by 4. For example, if you need 20 triangles, cut 5 squares twice diagonally.

When the shape is irregular and/or the size of the patch cannot easily be found on your rotary ruler, you'll need to make templates. Templates made for machine piecing include the ¼"-wide seam allowances.

1. Use removable tape to secure a piece of plastic template material on the template shapes indicated for each project. Trace the outside lines, using a ruler and pencil or fine-point permanent marker. Mark the identification letter and the straight-grain arrow on the plastic template. The marked side is the right side of the template. Cut out the template on the line. Confirm the accuracy of your template by placing it back on the drawing; you should be able to just see the printed line along the edge.

2. To trace the templates onto the fabric, place the template wrong side up on the wrong side of the fabric, making sure the straight-grain arrow is on the straight grain of the fabric. Trace around the template and cut out on the line.

Make Machine-Piecing Templates

The exception to the rule of placing the template wrong side up for tracing is when you need a reverse template, in which case you will place the template *right side up* on the wrong side of the fabric. You can also use the method described on page 92 to cut a reverse template.

You can use the edges of some template shapes as your cutting guide. This method was used to cut the trapezoid fabric pieces in "Home Sweet Home" (page 164).

1. Use double-stick tape or a washable gluestick to secure the template to the edge of the ruler. Make sure the straight-grain arrow is parallel to the ruler edge.

Attach Templates to the Ruler

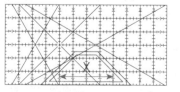

Attach template to ruler edge.

2. Place the ruler along the clean-cut edge of the fabric to cut a strip the width of the template. Cut the strip long enough to accommodate the number of pieces required.

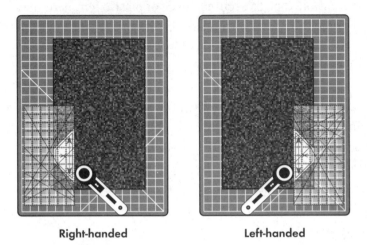

Right-handed   **Left-handed**

3. Remove the template and reattach it across the corner of the ruler. Place the template on the strip as shown and cut the two angles. Continue to cut additional pieces from the strip, aligning the already cut angle of the fabric with the edge of the ruler as shown. Pivot the ruler as you work your way down the strip.

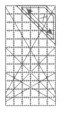

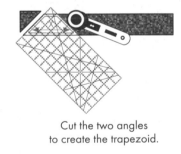

Attach the template across
the corner of the ruler.

Cut the two angles
to create the trapezoid.

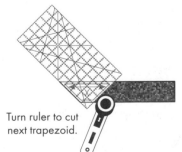

Turn ruler to cut
next trapezoid.

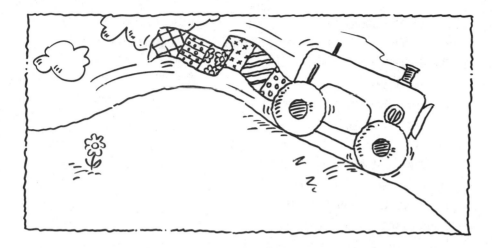

Learn Machine-Sewing Savvy

Since your sewing machine is the vehicle that will take you through the next phases of your patchwork, it needs to be in good working condition. You also need to feel comfortable with your machine. If you have never read the manual that came with your machine, now would be a good time to do so. If your machine leaves you frustrated because it doesn't work as it should, perhaps it is time to have it serviced or go shopping for a new machine that does make you happy. Life is short, and I firmly believe we should seek happiness!

Good sewing-machine hygiene can make the difference between smooth sewing and frustrating interruptions. Clean and oil your machine as directed in your manual. Change the needle after approximately eight hours of sewing. Use a size 80/12 needle and set the stitch length to about 12 stitches per inch.

Sewing a ¼"-Wide Seam Allowance

The single most important thing to remember when sewing your patches together is to sew with an exact ¼" seam allowance. If your seam allowance is as much as ¹⁄₁₆" off, you will be ¼" off after four seams, ½" after eight seams, and an entire inch off after sixteen seams.

I know it will be tempting to ignore the following test exercise, but I can't stress enough how important it is to your successful machine piecing. Since you will be joining fabric pieces that need to match other fabric pieces or pieced units, the accuracy of your seam allowance is crucial. It will make the difference between everything going along as planned or lots of frustration. *Please test your seam allowance.*

If you can change the needle position on your machine, move the needle so that it is ¼" from the right-hand edge of your presser foot.

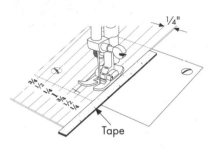

1. Place a rotary ruler under the presser foot, aligning the right edge of the ruler with the right edge of the presser foot.
2. Move the needle to the right one increment at a time until it is directly over the ¼" mark on the ruler. Gently lower the needle by hand to make sure.
3. Place several layers of masking tape along the edge of the ruler and presser foot.

If you cannot change the position of your needle, you can still make a ¼"-wide sewing guide.

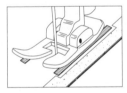

1. Place a rotary ruler under the presser foot and slowly drop the needle by hand until it hits the ¼" line on the ruler.
2. Place several layers of masking tape along the edge of the ruler. If the ¼" mark falls under the presser foot, you will need to cut a notch in the tape so it does not interfere with the presser foot or the feed dogs (those little teeth that pull the fabrics).

Test Exercise: Cut four strips of fabric, each 1½" x 3", and join the long sides. Press. The finished unit should measure *exactly* 4½" across. If needed, repeat this process, adjusting the tape guide or the needle position until you have established an accurate ¼"-wide seam guide. Smile and say to yourself, "Well done!"

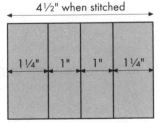

To sew patches together, place the fabric pieces right sides together. If you use 100% cotton fabric, the fabric pieces should adhere to each other, and straight-grain edges shouldn't stretch much. If it makes you feel more secure in the beginning, pin these pieces together. You can place the pins horizontally from the left or right or vertically—the choice is yours.

Sewing Patches

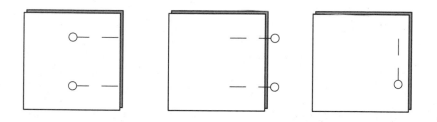

Since bias edges are more likely to stretch, be sure to pin pieces with bias edges until you gain a bit of experience.

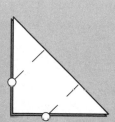

Press, then trim away the "dog ears" (those little protruding triangles) on joined units so they will not interfere when you sew.

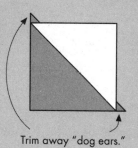

Trim away "dog ears."

Stitch ¼" from the edge, removing the pins as the needle approaches. Let the feed dogs feed, and don't tug on the fabric. Your job is to steer the fabric into the needle. To save time and thread, chain sew one seam right after the other without cutting the thread. This is also called fast feeding.

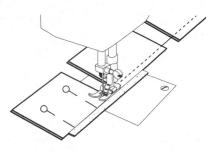

Matching Seam Intersections

Part of sewing accurately on the machine is matching seam intersections. To evenly distribute the seam allowances and eliminate bumpy intersections, press the seam allowances in opposite directions so they will "lock" into each other. When joining seams from two pieced units, butt the seams at the intersections.

Butt straight seams.   Butt diagonal seams.

Press the seam allowances away from points so the stitching lines of previously pieced units are visible. When you are joining pieces that require sewing across points, place the side with the points face up so you can see where to cross the seams.

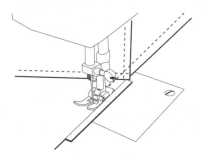

When joining two units that are seamed at the corner, begin sewing at the seamed corner for a good match.

Begin at this corner.

Machine basting important seam intersections saves time and eliminates frustration. Basting those important intersections ahead of time gives you an easy second chance to do it better if necessary. It also secures those areas so they will not move or shift when you stitch the seam for good. Trust me, it really works! Set the sewing machine to a long stitch and sew about 1" across the intersection. Check the intersection from the right side of the fabric to confirm a good match. If you are not pleased with the match, all you have to do is cut and pull the thread from the bobbin side of the mismatched seam and try again. When you are happy with all your intersections, sew the seam with your regular stitch length.

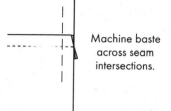

Basting Seam Intersections

Machine baste across seam intersections.

When several intersections fall along a seam line, simply pull the piece to the next intersection and machine baste.

Measure the first of each pieced unit along the way to make sure you are sewing the units together correctly and with the correct seam allowance. If you find something is not working out as it should, don't automatically assume you sewed with an incorrect seam allowance and try to make it work by easing it to the next unit. Stop and make sure the pieces are the correct size and shape. Perhaps you picked up the wrong fabric piece or sewed the wrong side of the patch. Get your ruler out and find out why the problem exists.

If you find, however, that one piece or unit is correct but just a bit oversized, you can ease it in. Place the unit that needs to be eased on the bottom, closest to the feed dogs. They will do a better job of easing in the fullness than you can. However, if the discrepancy is too large, cut another piece or redo the unit.

Troubleshooting

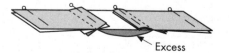

Excess

You will no doubt need to "unsew" something at some point. This is when your "unsewing tool" (better known as a seam ripper) will come in handy (see page 39).

Match Rotary-Cut Pieces

Since rotary-cut fabric pieces do not have the sewing line marked on them, it is important to place them together correctly before sewing. Some shapes are easy to match because they are the same shape and size. Sometimes, however, you will need to sew together two different shapes or different sizes of the same shape. It is important to know how to properly align the shapes. The following examples are shapes that you will encounter in the projects in this book. The diagram on the left shows how the joined shapes will appear when sewn. On the right, I have shown the two shapes with the ¼"-wide seam allowances properly positioned and ready to sew.

To join these: Do this:

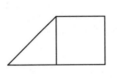
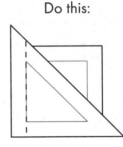

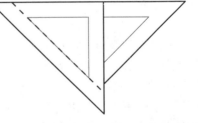

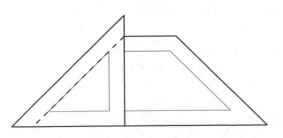

Matching Odd Shapes

One way to properly align different shapes is to mark the fabric at the finished end points of the seam line. Use a ⅛" hole punch to make holes in the templates at the seam intersections. With a pencil, mark the wrong side of the fabric pieces through the holes. Match the pencil marks on the pieces to be aligned and pin.

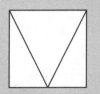

Shapes to be joined

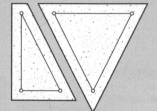

Holes punched in templates

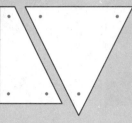

Fabric pieces marked

Fabric pieces correctly aligned and pinned

Strip piecing can be used when making several blocks consisting of squares and/or rectangles with the same fabrics. Strips of fabric are sewn together and crosscut into segments to create presewn patchwork combinations. For example, you can use strip piecing to cut and sew one of the blocks in "Simple Stars" (page 148). The finished size of the block is 10", and it consists of two different units.

Strip Piece by Machine

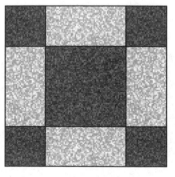

10" Plain Block

Unit A
(Two per block)

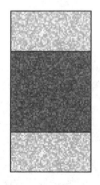

Unit B
(One per block)

Cut the fabric strips as directed and sew the strips together to make two different strip sets. Press the seam allowances for each strip set in opposite directions. Cut the strip sets into segments as directed. Sew two segments from strip set A to opposite sides of a segment from strip set B to complete each block.

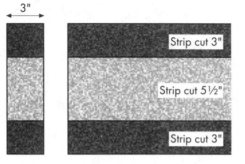

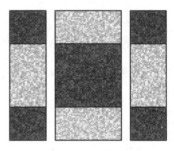

Strip Set A
Cut into 3" segments.

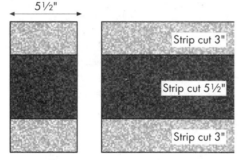

Strip Set B
Cut into 5½" segments.

Machine Piecing on Your Own

The machine-piecing information presented so far is enough to get you through the beginner projects in this book. The following information will help you when you are ready to go on and machine piece patchwork on your own.

- If you are going to machine piece a block you have drawn, look for the easiest combination of patches to make the block with no set-in seams (see page 60). (Set-in seams can be sewn on the sewing machine, but this technique is not usually tackled by beginners.) List how many and what size squares, rectangles, and triangles to rotary cut. The cut size is the finished size of the patch plus ¼"-wide seam allowances on all sides.

- To determine the cut size for simple shapes, use the following guide.

Squares: Add ½" to the finished size.

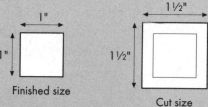

Rectangles: Add ½" to the finished length and width.

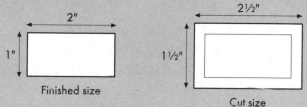

Half-square triangles: Add ⅞" to the finished short side of the triangle. Cut a square that size and cut it once diagonally to make 2 half-square triangles.

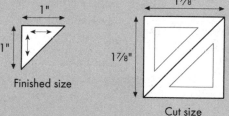

Quarter-square triangles: Add 1¼" to the finished long side of the triangle. Cut a square that size and cut it twice diagonally to make 4 quarter-square triangles.

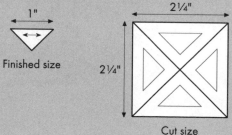

Continued on page 92

- If you need to make templates for other shapes, add the ¼"-wide seam allowance to all sides of the finished size. To do this, trace the finished-size shape on plastic template material. Place the ¼" line on your ruler on one side of the finished shape. Draw along the ruler's edge to add the ¼"-wide seam allowance. Repeat with all sides of the shape. Cut the shape on the outside line.
- Attach the template to the ruler to cut pieces when you can (see pages 81–82). Otherwise, place the wrong side of the template face up on the *wrong* side of the fabric and trace around the shape. *Cut on the line.* Remember to align the straight-grain arrow with the straight grain of the fabric.
- If you need to cut a template and its reverse, you can cut both pieces at the same time. Simply layer your fabric right sides together, mark your fabric, and cut. You will end up with two pieces, one of which will be reversed.

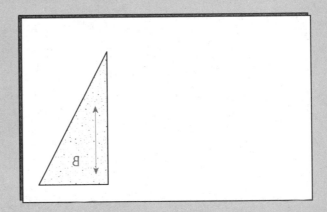

Fabrics layered right sides together

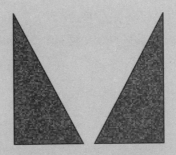

The Pillow

By Carol Doak, 1996, Windham, New Hampshire, 12" x 12" (without 2¼"-wide ruffle). If you aren't ready to jump into making a quilt yet, this pillow is an easy introduction to both pieced patchwork and quilting and makes a delightful accent for any room. Directions begin on page 108.

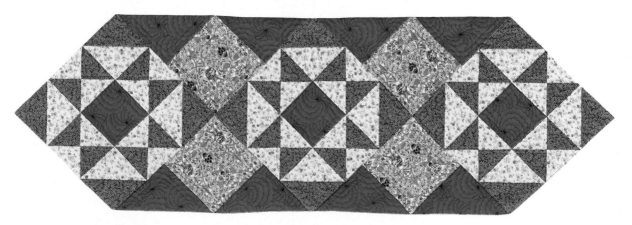

The Table Runner

By Carol Doak, 1996, Windham, New Hampshire, 17" x 51". Sample several different patchwork techniques and, at the same time, make something that will brighten any table. Simple straight-line quilting accents the patchwork shapes. Directions begin on page 116.

Flower Pots

By Carol Doak, 1996, Windham, New Hampshire, 38¾" x 38¾". Use a large-scale fabric in the alternate block and setting triangles to establish a color theme for your own Flower Pot quilt. Only four Flower Pot blocks are in this quilt, and it is a great introduction to making a quilt that is set on-point. The crosshatch quilting in the side triangles, corner triangles, and alternate block creates an interesting texture. A decorative floral design fills the border. Directions begin on page 124.

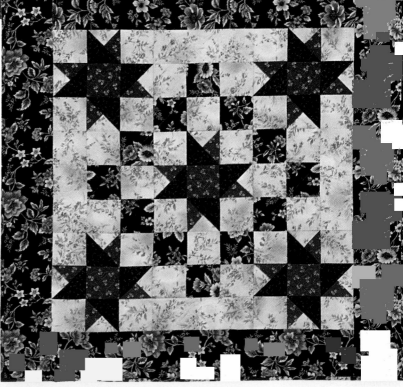

Star Bright

By Carol Doak, 1996, Windham, New Hampshire, 36½" x 36½". Whether you piece it by hand or machine, this is a great first quilt. The alternate blocks offer the opportunity to try machine strip piecing. The subtle quality of the background fabric suggests just a bit of movement. Quilted hearts decorate the patchwork blocks, and the straight lines through the center squares accentuate the frame around the center star. Machine quilted by Ellen Peters. Directions begin on page 132.

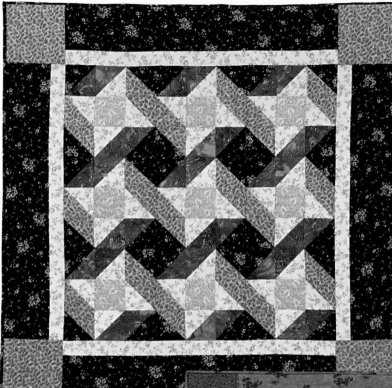

Ribbons

By Carol Doak, 1996, Windham, New Hampshire, 39½" x 39½". Although this quilt is made from nine identical blocks, the effect it produces is intriguing. Straight lines of quilting accentuate the woven effect of this quilt and are continued in the corner squares. A gentle, soft cable in the outer border emphasizes the woven theme. Machine quilted by Ellen Peters. Directions begin on page 141.

Simple Stars

By Carol Doak, 1996, Windham, New Hampshire, 40½" x 40½". The impact of the two simple four patch designs is striking. You can piece these blocks easily by hand, or you can use quick strip-piecing methods. The machine stipple quilting in the white center area is a wonderful attention-getter! A circle of hearts decorates the center squares of the plain blocks, and a single heart is featured in the center square of the Sawtooth Star. The outer border features a vine design on the top and crosshatching on the other three sides. Who says all four borders have to be quilted identically? Machine quilted by Ellen Peters. Directions begin on page 148.

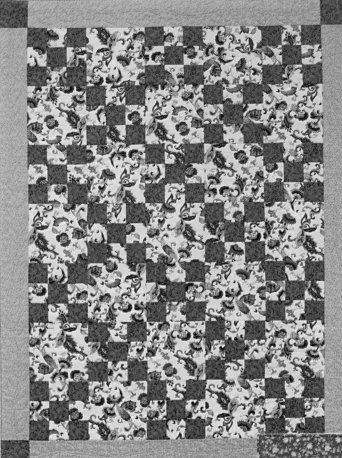

Single Irish Chain
By Carol Doak, 1996,
Windham, New Hampshire, 36½" x 48½".
The large areas in the alternating blocks
in this quilt offer the opportunity to feature a
fabric with a favorite color combination
or to set a theme. Hanging on the wall or
draped over a chair, this quilt would add a
spark to any room. It is also an ideal little
quilt for a special someone. It is easy to
hand piece on the go or machine piece in a
jiffy, using strip-piecing methods. Simple
straight-line quilting in the patchwork
blocks and quarter circles in the alternating
blocks can be done easily by hand or
machine. The border features a simple
but elegant leaf vine that meanders around
the patchwork center. Machine quilted by
Ellen Peters. Directions begin on page 157.

Home Sweet Home
By Carol Doak, 1996,
Windham, New Hampshire, 32½" x 32½".
This quilt contains some of my favorite patchwork
pictures. It evokes a lovely thought and is sure
to warm any home or heart. Since there are
three different block designs, you'll have a chance
to try several new techniques in this small wall
quilt. Stipple quilting creates texture in the trees,
and the Heart blocks are simply crosshatched
through the squares. Straight lines add detail
to the roof of the house, and the border features a
hearts-and-flowers vine to continue the sentiment
of the quilt. Machine quilted by Ellen Peters.
Directions begin on page 164.

Pressing Your Patchwork (it's much easier than shirts!)

When hand piecing, finger-press the sewn units as they are stitched. When the block is completed, press the seam allowances flat. The general rule is to press seam allowances to the darker side of the patchwork in a consistent fashion. However, if pressing this way creates excess bulk, you may press in an alternate fashion, such as pressing seam allowances away from points. Be sure to press your completed block carefully so you don't distort it. Use an up-and-down motion instead of dragging the iron across the fabric, and do not use steam.

When machine piecing, press each seam after you stitch so the seam allowances go in opposite directions and butt at intersections. A small travel iron next to your machine and a pressing pad is efficient. You can also lower the ironing board next to your machine to press without ever having to get up. First, press the line of stitching from the wrong side of the fabric to set the seam and relax the stitching, then use the tip of the iron as shown to press the fabric over the seam allowance.

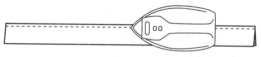

Press the stitching.

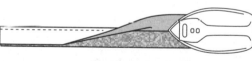

Press the seam.

If you fast-feed your patchwork (see page 85), you can fast-press it too! Lay the strip of pieced units on the ironing board. Press the line of stitching first, then press the patches open. Clip the threads to separate the units.

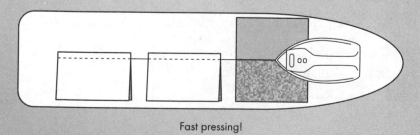

Fast pressing!

The Setting Pieces

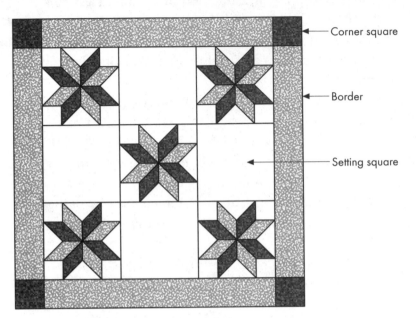

Corner square

Border

Setting square

Quilt Set with Alternate Blocks

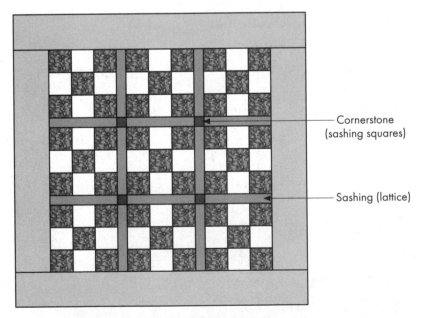

Cornerstone
(sashing squares)

Sashing (lattice)

Quilt Set with Sashing and Cornerstones

Fabric pieces such as borders, corner squares, setting blocks, setting triangles, sashings, and cornerstones are often joined to the blocks to complete the quilt top. These are referred to as setting pieces, and they, too, need to be cut the finished size plus a ½" total for seam allowances.

For hand piecing: If you have several small setting pieces to mark and cut, make a template for the finished dimension of the setting piece. Mark and cut it as you did your other templates. For larger pieces, you have two options:

- You can mark the finished size of the piece on the wrong side of the fabric and cut it out ¼" from the sewing line.
- You can rotary cut the pieces with the ½" total for seam allowances already included, then mark the sewing line ¼" from the perimeter on all sides. This is really the easier method when cutting large setting triangles and is used for cutting the side and corner triangles in "Flower Pots" (page 124).

For machine piecing: Use your rotary cutter and ruler to cut the setting pieces, including ¼" for each seam allowance (½" total).

Quilts set on-point (blocks placed on the diagonal) have two types of setting triangles. The side triangles are quarter-square triangles with the straight grain on the long side of the triangle. The corner triangles are half-square triangles with the straight grain on the short side of the triangle. See pages 79–80 to learn more about quarter-square and half-square triangles.

Alternate setting squares are usually cut on the straight grain so you won't have long bias edges. You can cut them on the bias if you desire. For instance, if you are using a directional fabric such as a plaid, and you want it to run vertically and horizontally in the on-point quilt, you will need to cut the square on the bias. The bias edges will be secured by the straight-grain edges of the pieced blocks.

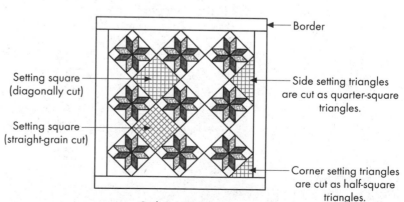

Border

Setting square
(diagonally cut)

Side setting triangles
are cut as quarter-square
triangles.

Setting square
(straight-grain cut)

Corner setting triangles
are cut as half-square
triangles.

Quilt Set On-Point

Calculating Setting Triangles (no problem)

Here are some simple truths:

- Multiplying the side of a square by 1.4142 gives you the diagonal measurement of the square.
- Multiplying the short side of a setting triangle by 1.4142 gives you the length of the long side of the triangle.
- Dividing the long side of a setting triangle by 1.4142 gives you the length of the short side of the triangle.

Oh, I realize that math might not be your thing! Therefore, I strongly suggest all calculations be done on a calculator. Of course, when dealing with a calculator, you need to convert decimals to inches and round off to the nearest ⅛". The following chart converts decimals to fractions.

.125	=	⅛"	.625	=	⅝"
.25	=	¼"	.75	=	¾"
.375	=	⅜"	.875	=	⅞"
.50	=	½"	1.0	=	1"

SIDE TRIANGLES

To find out what size square(s) to cut to make the side triangles, you need to find out the length of the long side of the triangle and add 1¼" for seam allowances. Remember, the straight grain needs to be on the long side of the side triangle (a quarter-square triangle). Let's work with a 12" finished block size as an example.

Step One: Since the short side of the side triangle adjoins the side of the finished 12" block, we know that the finished length of the triangle's short side is 12". Multiply 12" (the length of the short side) by 1.4142 to find the finished length of the triangle's long side. The calculator says the answer is 16.97". Round up to the nearest ⅛". Therefore, the length of the finished long side of the triangle is 17".

Step Two: Now we just need to add the seam allowances to this measurement. For quarter-square triangles, you add 1¼" to the finished measurement of the triangle's long side to determine the size of the square to cut. Therefore, 1¼" plus 17" equals 18¼". Cut a square 18¼" x 18¼" and cut it twice diagonally to yield four side triangles.

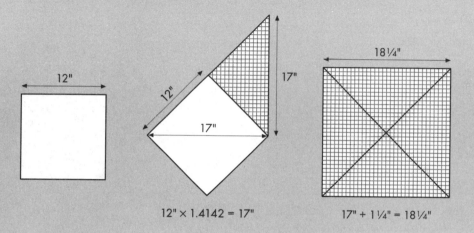

12"

12"   17"

17"

18¼"

12" × 1.4142 = 17"   17" + 1¼" = 18¼"

CORNER TRIANGLES

To find the size of the squares to cut for the corner triangles, you need to find out the length of the triangle's short side and add ⅞" for seam allowances. Remember, the straight grain needs to be on the short side of the triangle (a half-square triangle). Let's use the same 12" finished block size as an example.

Step One: Since the finished long side of the corner triangle adjoins the side of the 12" block, we know that the finished length of the triangle's long side is 12". Divide 12" by 1.4142 to find the finished length of the corner triangle's short side. The calculator says the answer is 8.485362749. OK, I admit it. I got a little carried away with the calculator. Anyway, round this up to 8½".

Continued on page 102

Step Two: Now add the seam allowances to this measurement. For half-square triangles, you add ⅞" to the finished measurement of the triangle's short side to determine the size of the square to cut. Therefore, ⅞" plus 8½" equals 9⅜". Cut two 9⅜" squares once diagonally to make the four corner triangles.

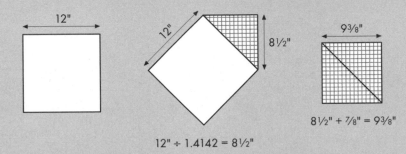

12" ÷ 1.4142 = 8½"

8½" + ⅞" = 9⅜"

Is this giving you a headache? It's OK. Just refer to the handy chart below to determine the finished diagonal size of a variety of finished block sizes and the size of the squares to cut for the corner and side triangles. For example, if your quilt blocks are 6" finished, they would measure 8½" diagonally. To make the corner triangles, cut 5⅛" squares once diagonally (half-square triangles). To make the side triangles, cut 9¾" squares twice diagonally (quarter-square triangles).

Finished Square Size	Finished Diagonal Size	Cut Square Size for Corner Triangles	Cut Square Size for Side Triangles
5"	7⅛"	4½"	8⅜"
6"	8½"	5⅛"	9¾"
7"	9⅞"	5⅞"	11¼"
8"	11⅜"	6⅝"	12⅝"
9"	12¾"	7¼"	14"
10"	14⅛"	8"	15½"
11"	15½"	8¾"	16⅞"
12"	17"	9⅜"	18¼"
13"	18⅜"	10⅛"	19⅝"
14"	19⅞"	10¾"	21⅛"
15"	21¼"	11½"	22½"
16"	22⅝"	12¼"	23⅞"

Once the blocks are completed, it is time to assemble the quilt top. The projects in this book are set straight in a grid fashion or diagonally on-point.

Place your blocks side by side in rows. Pin and sew the blocks together in horizontal rows. Press the seams in opposite directions from row to row. Sew the rows together, making sure to match the seams between each block.

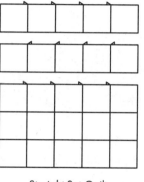

Straight-Set Quilt

Place your blocks on the diagonal, or on-point. This type of setting requires setting triangles to fill in the spaces around the edges of the quilt. Remember, the triangles along the sides are quarter-square triangles, and the triangles on the corners are half-square triangles. Sew the rows together diagonally and press the seams in opposite directions from row to row. Sew the rows together, making sure to match the seams between each block. Add the corner triangles last.

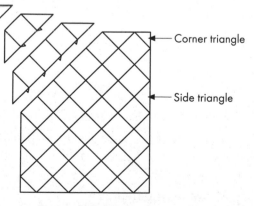

Diagonally Set Quilt

Assembling the Quilt Top

Set Blocks Straight

Set Blocks Diagonally

Borders: Keeping It Together

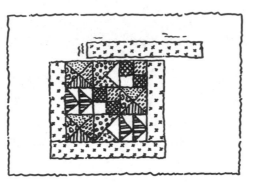

Once the center portion of your project is complete, it is time to add borders. The measurements for borders are provided with each project. It is a good idea, however, to check the size of your completed quilt top and make any necessary adjustments, since your quilt could grow or shrink slightly. Even if you hand pieced the patchwork blocks, consider sewing the borders on by machine.

The borders for the projects in this book either have straight-cut corners or corner squares. Another option is to miter the corners of the border strips. In our effort to narrow the focus of this book to a couple of options, we are not addressing mitered corners.

- If your cut border length is 21" or less, cut two borders at a time across the folded fabric width.
- If your cut border length is between 22" and 40", cut one border at a time across the width of a single layer of fabric.
- If your cut border length is more than 40", cut two borders at a time along the length of a double layer of fabric.

Borders that ruffle around the center portion of the quilt are a common ailment. Two things will help you avoid the situation. The first is to measure your quilt top through its center rather than along the edges to determine the border measurement. The second is to pin your borders well before sewing them.

1. Measure the *length* of the quilt top (from top to bottom) through the center, from raw edge to raw edge, and cut two border strips to this measurement. Mark the centers of the border strips and the quilt top. Pin the border strips to the sides, matching the center marks and ends. Pin the rest of the border, easing as necessary. Sew and press the seams toward the border strips.

Make Borders with Straight-Cut Corners

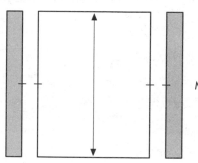

Mark centers.

Measure center of quilt, top to bottom.

2. Measure the *width* of the quilt top (from side to side) through the center, from raw edge to raw edge, including the border pieces you just added; cut two border strips to this measurement. Mark the centers of the border strips and the quilt top. Pin the border strips to the top and bottom edges, matching the center marks and ends. Pin the rest of the border, easing as necessary. Sew and press the seams toward the border strips.

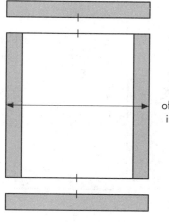

Measure center of quilt, side to side, including borders.

Mark centers.

If desired, you may add the border strips to the top and bottom edges first and then to the sides. Isn't it great to have choices? If you choose this option, measure the quilt vertically first, and then horizontally.

Make Borders with Corner Squares

1. Cut 2 side borders to match the center length measurement. Cut top and bottom borders to match the center width measurement. Pin and sew the border strips to opposite *sides* of the quilt top first, then press the seams toward the border.

If your quilt has more than one border, sew the individual strips together and treat as one unit before adding the corner squares.

2. Attach the corner squares to the top and bottom strips and press the seams toward the border strips. Pin and sew these strips to the top and bottom edges of the quilt top. Press the seams toward the border.

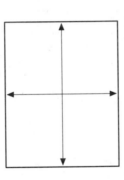
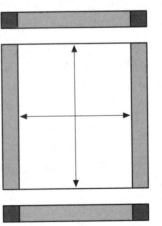

Just to make sure those corner seams match properly, machine baste the intersecting seams at the corners after pinning the top and bottom borders in place. See page 87.

Beginner Projects

Can we talk? I want to share a few thoughts with you. These projects were specifically designed with you, the beginner, in mind. I assumed you would not have a large fabric stash, so you don't need a lot of different fabrics to make these projects.

Each project begins with an illustration of the layout and pertinent information about the size of the quilt, blocks, and borders in the "Project Information at a Glance." The amount needed for each fabric is listed. The blocks used in the projects are shown with and without grids so you can see how the block was created. The template letters are indicated in each design so you know where the cut pieces will be placed. Finally, the design is exploded to show the piecing sequence.

The icon on the left, below, will alert you to hand-piecing information. The icon on the right will alert you to machine-piecing information:

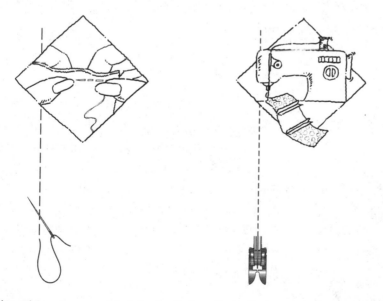

Directions are provided for both hand piecing and rotary cutting each of the projects. If you are hand piecing and would rather rotary cut the setting pieces (the borders, etc.), you can cut these pieces according to the "size to cut" column in the cutting chart and mark your sewing line ¼" from the edge (see page 98).

The piecing sequence for both hand and machine piecing will be the same for most of the patchwork. When it is different, such as the machine strip piecing in "Star Bright," "Simple Stars," and "Single Irish Chain," the directions are separated for the two options. If you are machine piecing, those little one-sided arrows will let you know which way to press the seam allowances so they'll go in opposite directions (see page 86).

Remember Henry Ford and his assembly line? You can assemble the units in the step-by-step directions in the same way. For example, the table runner requires 3 blocks. Step 1 directs you to make 4 units for 1 block. To make all the units for all 3 blocks, make 12 of these units one right after the other. You will be multiplying each step times 3 to make your 3 blocks in assembly-line fashion.

The directions for completing the pillow and table runner are given with the projects. For the quilts, refer to the general directions on pages 175–208 to complete your project. I have included quilting suggestions for each of the projects, but feel free to let yourself go and do something different. The quilting designs used in "Simple Stars," "Ribbons," "Star Bright," and "Single Irish Chain" are provided on pages 217–20.

Most of all, relax and have fun!

The Pillow

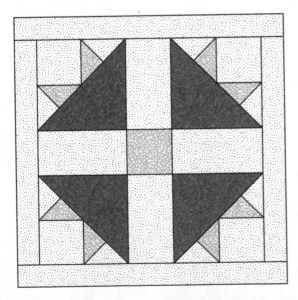

Someone once said to me that a quilt is only a number of pillows. If you are at all intimidated about starting your quilting journey, then perhaps this pillow is the place to start. It is a good introduction to patchwork. The single block can be easily pieced by hand or machine, but you will want to use a sewing machine to construct the pillow once the block is completed.

Project Information at a Glance

Finished Pillow Size:	12" x 12" (without 2¼"-wide ruffle)
Name of Block:	Cross and Crown
Finished Block Size:	10" x 10"
Patchwork Grid:	Five patch
Number of Blocks to Make:	1
Finished Border Width:	1"

Materials: 44"-wide fabric

¼ yd. green print (includes setting pieces)

⅛ yd. red print

⅝ yd. multicolored black print for block, ruffle, and back of pillow

14" x 14" square of muslin for inside backing of patchwork square*

14" x 14" square of low-loft batting

12" x 12" pillow form

4 safety pins

 Green print

 Red print

 Multicolored print

*The backing of the patchwork square will be inside the pillow and will not be seen. Therefore, muslin or any other light-colored woven cotton fabric can be used.

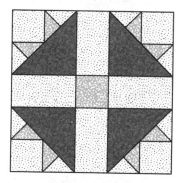

Cross and Crown Block
Make 1.

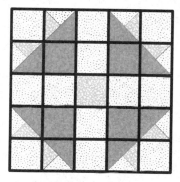

Five-patch grid

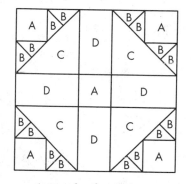

Letters identify templates and rotary-cut pieces.

Cutting

Setting Pieces				
FABRIC	NO. OF PIECES	SIZE TO MARK	SIZE TO CUT	PLACEMENT
Green	2	1" x 10"	1½" x 10½"	side borders
	2	1" x 12"	1½" x 12½"	top/bottom borders

Block Pieces to Mark and Cut		

Make templates A, B, C, and D (page 210).
Don't forget to add ¼"-wide seam allowances when cutting pieces.

FABRIC	NO. OF PIECES	TEMPLATE
Green	4	A
	8	B
	4	D
Red	1	A
	8	B
Black	4	C

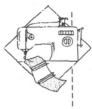

Cutting

Setting Pieces			
FABRIC	NO. OF PIECES	SIZE TO ROTARY CUT	PLACEMENT
Green	2	1½" x 10½"	side borders
	2	1½" x 12½"	top/bottom borders

Block Pieces to Rotary Cut					
FABRIC	NO. OF PIECES	1ST CUT	2ND CUT	YIELD	PLACEMENT
Green	4	2½" x 2½"			A
	2	3¼" x 3¼"	⊠	8	B
	4	2½" x 4½"			D
Red	1	2½" x 2½"			A
	2	3¼" x 3¼"	⊠	8	B
Black	2	4⅞" x 4⅞"	▨	4	C

⊠ Cut the squares twice diagonally.
▨ Cut the squares once diagonally.

Block Assembly

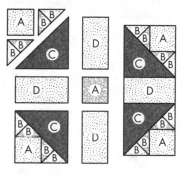

1. Join 1 green triangle (B) and 1 red triangle (B) as shown.

Make 4.

2. Join 1 green triangle (B) and 1 red triangle (B) as shown.

Make 4.

3. Sew a triangle unit from step 1 to the bottom of a green square (A).

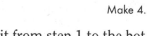

Make 4.

4. Sew a unit from step 2 to the right side of the pieced unit from step 3.

Make 4.

5. Sew a black triangle (C) to the pieced unit from step 4. Psst…if you are machine piecing, don't forget to pin these pieces together first, because they might stretch as you sew across the bias edges. Sew with the pieced portion facing up so you can be sure to cross the stitching at the right location in the center (see page 86).

Make 4.

6. Join 2 units from step 5 and a green rectangle (D) to make a row.

 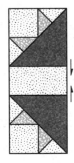

Make 2.

7. Sew a green rectangle (D) to each side of a red square (A) to make the center row.

Make 1.

8. Join the rows to complete the block.

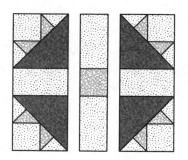 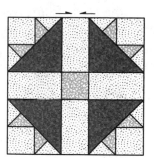

Hooray!

Pillow Assembly and Finishing

1. Sew a 1½" x 10½" (cut size) green strip to opposite sides of the block. Sew a 1½" x 12½" (cut size) green strip to the top and bottom of the block.

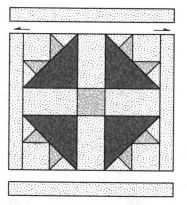 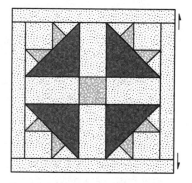

2. Layer the patchwork block, 14" x 14" batting square, and 14" x 14" muslin square; baste (see pages 185–86). Quilt the square by hand or by machine.

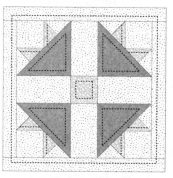

Quilting Suggestion

3. When the quilting is completed, machine or hand baste ⅛" from the edge of the patchwork; trim the batting and backing fabric even with the edge of the patchwork pillow.

4. From the black print, cut 2 strips, each 5" wide, across the width of the fabric from selvage to selvage. Join the strips on the short ends. Press the seams open. With wrong sides together, fold the strip in half lengthwise and press. Fold the ring of fabric in half and then in quarters; mark the quarters with a safety pin. Hand or machine baste 2 rows of stitching, ⅛" and ¼" from the cut edge.

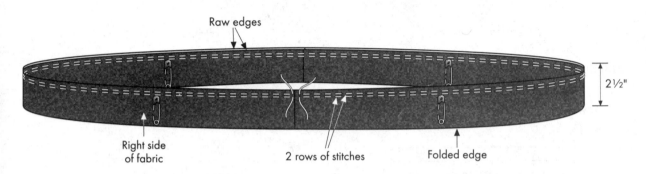

Raw edges

Right side of fabric

2 rows of stitches

Folded edge

2½"

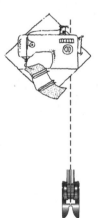

5. Pull the thread to gather each quarter section to fit each side of the pillow. Pin the 4 safety pins in the 4 corners of the pillow top, placing the cut edge of the ruffle even with the edge of the pillow. Distribute the ruffles evenly, adding a bit of extra fullness in the corners. Machine stitch ¼" from the edge.

If you machine basted the gathering stitches, pull the bobbin thread to gather the ruffle. It's usually a bit looser and therefore easier to pull.

6. From the black print, cut 2 rectangles, each 9" x 12½". Along one long side of each black rectangle, turn under ¼" twice; press and machine stitch to create a finished edge.

Wrong side of black print

Make 2.

7. With right sides together, place one rectangle on top of the pillow and ruffle. Pin in place. Place the other rectangle, right side down, on top of the unit as shown. Pin in place. Machine stitch around the perimeter of the pillow, using a generous ¼"-wide seam allowance.

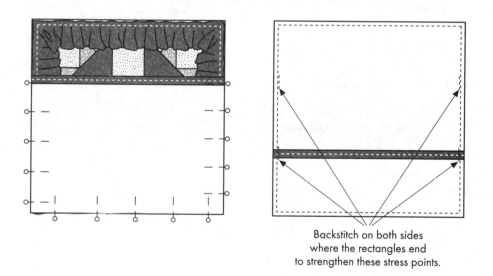

Backstitch on both sides
where the rectangles end
to strengthen these stress points.

8. Turn the pillow right side out. Insert a 12" x 12" pillow form.

The Table Runner

Making this table runner is another good introduction to quiltmaking. The three Four X blocks and four Four Patch half blocks are easy to make by hand or machine.

Project Information at a Glance		
Finished Runner Size:	17" x 51"	
Name of Block:	Four X	Four Patch half blocks
Finished Block Size:	12" x 12"	12" (short sides)
Patchwork Grid:	Nine patch	Four patch
Number of Blocks to Make:	3	4

 Light green print

 Dark green print

 Light pink print

 Medium pink print

Materials: 44"-wide fabric

¼ yd. light green print

1¼ yds. dark green print (includes backing)

½ yd. light pink print

½ yd. medium pink print

18" x 52" muslin for inside backing

18" x 52" batting

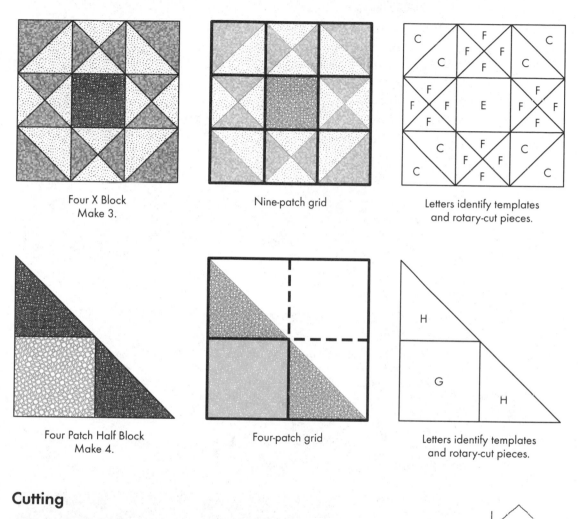

Four X Block
Make 3.

Nine-patch grid

Letters identify templates
and rotary-cut pieces.

Four Patch Half Block
Make 4.

Four-patch grid

Letters identify templates
and rotary-cut pieces.

Cutting

Backing			
Cut strips from selvage to selvage across the width of the fabric.			
FABRIC	NO. OF PIECES	SIZE TO MARK	SIZE TO CUT
Dark green	2	17½" x 26½"	18" x 27"*
*The backing pieces are cut wider than the runner to allow for some fullness.			

Block Pieces to Mark and Cut

Make templates C, E, F, G and H (pages 210–12).
Don't forget to add ¼"-wide seam allowances when cutting pieces.

FABRIC	NO. OF PIECES	TEMPLATE
Light green	4	G
Dark green	8	H
	3	E
Light pink	12	C
	24	F
Medium pink	12	C
	24	F

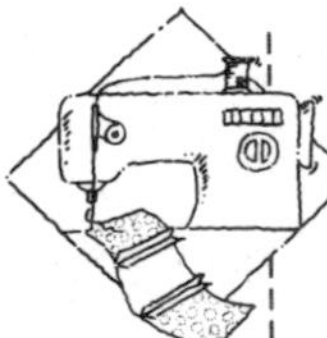

Cutting

Backing

Cut strips from selvage to selvage across the width of the fabric.

FABRIC	NO. OF PIECES	SIZE TO ROTARY CUT
Dark green	2	18" x 27"*

*The backing pieces are cut wider than the runner to allow for some fullness.

Block Pieces to Rotary Cut

FABRIC	NO. OF PIECES	1ST CUT	2ND CUT	YIELD	PLACEMENT
Light green	4	6½" x 6½"			G
Dark green	2	9¾" x 9¾"	⊠	8	H
	3	4½" x 4½"			E
Light pink	6	4⅞" x 4⅞"	◹	12	C
	6	5¼" x 5¼"	⊠	24	F
Medium pink	6	4⅞" x 4⅞"	◹	12	C
	6	5¼" x 5¼"	⊠	24	F

⊠ Cut the squares twice diagonally.
◹ Cut the squares once diagonally.

Block Assembly

Four X Blocks

The following directions are for making 1 Four X block. You can make 1 block at a time or all 3 blocks in assembly-line fashion.

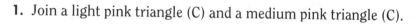
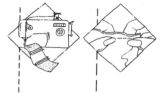

1. Join a light pink triangle (C) and a medium pink triangle (C).

Make 4.

2. Join a light pink triangle (F) and a medium pink triangle (F).

Make 8.

3. Join 2 units from step 2 as shown.

Make 4.

4. Join 2 units from step 1 and a unit from step 3 to make a row.

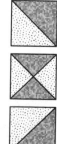

Make 2.

5. Join 2 units from step 3 and a dark green square (E) to make the center row.

Make 1.

6. Join the rows to complete the block.

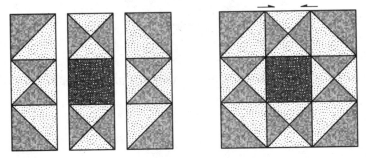

Hooray!

Half Blocks

The following directions are for making 1 half block. You can make 1 half block at a time or all 4 half blocks in assembly-line fashion.

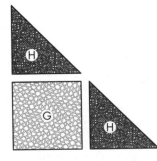

1. Join a light green square (G) and a dark green triangle (H).

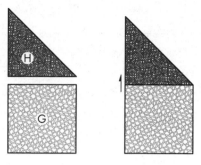

Make 1.

2. Add another dark green triangle (H) to the unit from step 1.

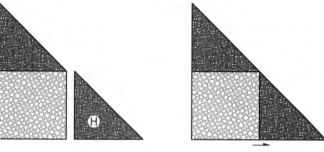

Hooray!

Table Runner Assembly and Finishing

1. Assemble the 3 blocks and 4 half blocks in diagonal rows as shown. Join the rows.

2. Layer the runner with the batting and muslin. Baste the 3 layers together (see pages 185–86). Quilt by hand or machine.

Batting

Muslin backing

Quilting Suggestion

3. Machine baste ⅛" from the edge of the patchwork. Trim the backing and batting flush with the patchwork runner.

4. Hem one short end of each 18" x 27" dark green backing piece. Turn under ¼" twice; press and machine stitch to create a finished edge.

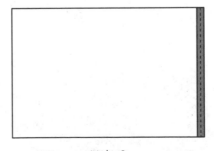

Make 2.

5. With the finished edge toward the center, pin 1 backing piece right sides together with the quilted runner, leaving just a bit of fullness across the width. With right sides together, pin the remaining backing piece at the other end of the runner, letting the finished edge overlap the other piece a few inches. Trim the runner backing flush with the quilted patchwork.

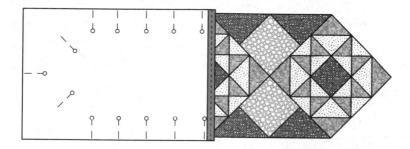

Back of quilted runner

6. Sew ¼" from the edges all around. Clip ¼" from the points to reduce bulk. Turn the runner right side out, pushing out the seams. Press lightly.

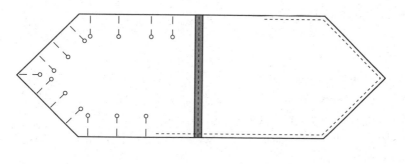

Flower Pots

There are only four pieced blocks in this wall quilt, and they are set on-point. This means that you will have a few long bias edges to sew when you add the side setting triangles and corner triangles. But it will be OK. Just be sure to pin those edges if you are going to machine piece this wall quilt.

Project Information at a Glance

Finished Quilt Size:	38¾" x 38¾"
Name of Block:	Flower Pot
Finished Block Size:	10" x 10"
Patchwork Grid:	Five patch
Number of Blocks to Make:	4
Finished Border Width:	5"

Large-scale print

Light blue print

Medium blue print

Pink print

Materials: 44"-wide fabric

⅝ yd. large-scale print

½ yd. light blue print

1¼ yds. medium blue print (includes border and binding)

¼ yd. pink print

1½ yds. for backing (includes 12" for sleeve)

42" x 42" square of batting

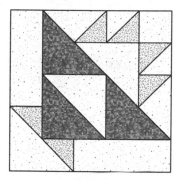

Flower Pot Block
Make 4.

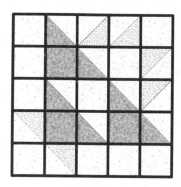

Five-patch grid

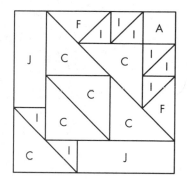

Letters identify templates
and rotary-cut pieces

Cutting

Setting Pieces

Even if you are hand piecing this quilt, I suggest you rotary cut the setting pieces since they are so large. *The seam allowances are included in the following measurements for the setting pieces. Mark the sewing line ¼" from the cut edges.* This is easier than making templates for these larger pieces.

Cut strips from selvage to selvage across the width of the fabric.

FABRIC	NO. OF PIECES	1ST ROTARY CUT	2ND ROTARY CUT	YIELD	PLACEMENT
Large-scale print	1	15½" x 15½"	⊠	4	side triangles
	2	8" x 8"	⊡	4	corner triangles
	1	10½" x 10½"			center square
Medium blue	2	5½" x 28¾"			side borders
	2	5½" x 38¾"			top/bottom borders

⊠ Cut the squares twice diagonally.
⊡ Cut the squares once diagonally.

Block Pieces to Mark and Cut

Make templates A, C, F, I and J (pages 210–12).
Don't forget to add ¼"-wide seam allowances when cutting pieces.

FABRIC	NO. OF PIECES	TEMPLATE
Light blue	4	A
	12	C
	8	F
	8	I
	8	J
Medium blue	12	C
Pink	24	I

Cutting

Setting Pieces

Cut strips from selvage to selvage across the width of the fabric.

FABRIC	NO. OF PIECES	1ST ROTARY CUT	2ND ROTARY CUT	YIELD	PLACEMENT
Large-scale print	1	15½" x 15½"	⊠	4	side triangles
	2	8" x 8"	◩	4	corner triangles
	1	10½" x 10½"			center square
Medium blue	2	5½" x 28¾"			side borders
	2	5½" x 38¾"			top/bottom borders

⊠ Cut the squares twice diagonally.
◩ Cut the squares once diagonally.

Block Pieces to Rotary Cut

FABRIC	NO. OF PIECES	1ST CUT	2ND CUT	YIELD	PLACEMENT
Light blue	4	2½" x 2½"			A
	6	4⅞" x 4⅞"	◹	12	C
	2	5¼" x 5¼"	⊠	8	F
	4	2⅞" x 2⅞"	◹	8	I
	8	2½" x 6½"			J
Medium blue	6	4⅞" x 4⅞"	◹	12	C
Pink	12	2⅞" x 2⅞"	◹	24	I

⊠ Cut the squares twice diagonally.
◹ Cut the squares once diagonally.

Block Assembly

The following directions are for making 1 Flower Pot block. You can make 1 block at a time or all 4 blocks in assembly-line fashion.

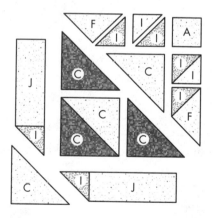

1. Join a pink triangle (I) and a light blue triangle (I).

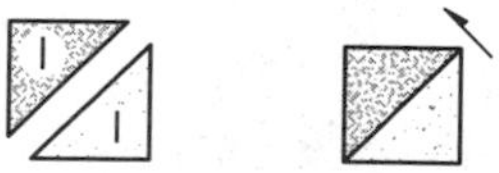

Make 2.

2. Join a pink triangle (I) and a light blue triangle (F) as shown to make 2 different units.

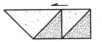

Make 1.   Make 1.

3. Join the units from steps 1 and 2 as shown to make 2 different units.

4. Sew a light blue square (A) to 1 unit from step 3 and a light blue triangle (C) to the other unit as shown. Join the 2 units to make the top section of the block.

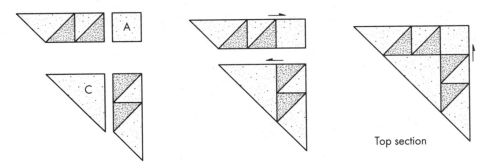

Top section

5. Join a light blue triangle (C) and a medium blue triangle (C). Add 2 medium blue triangles (C) as shown to make the bottom section of the block.

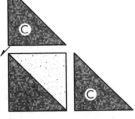
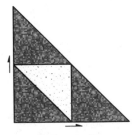

Bottom section

6. Join the top and bottom sections. Because you will be stitching across bias edges that stretch easily, be sure to securely pin the sections before sewing.

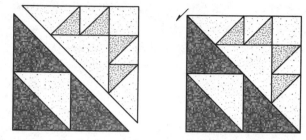

7. Join a light blue rectangle (J) and a pink triangle (I) as shown to make 2 different units.

Make 1.   Make 1.

8. Join the units from step 7 to the unit from step 6 as shown. Complete the block by adding the light blue triangle (C).

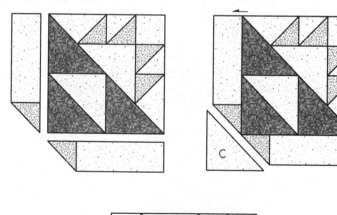

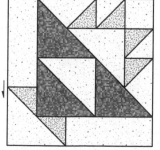

Hooray!

Quilt Top Assembly

1. Arrange the blocks and setting pieces as shown below.
2. Since the bias edges of the triangles stretch easily, pin, then sew together the corner units. Attach the side triangles first and then the corner triangles. Pin and sew together the center row. Join the corner units and center row to complete the center patchwork section. Remember to pin wherever you have bias edges.

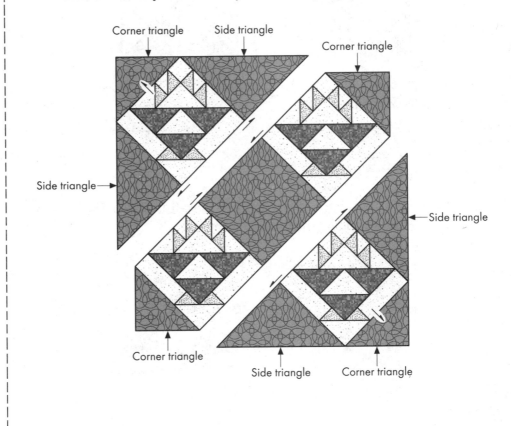

3. Sew border strips to the sides of the center patchwork section first, then to the top and bottom to complete the quilt top.

4. Refer to pages 175–208 for directions on finishing your quilt.

Quilting Suggestion

Star Bright

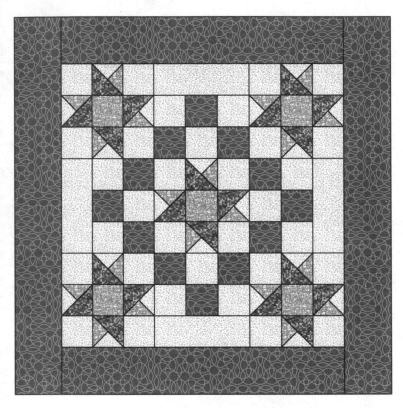

This wall quilt is easy to make by hand or machine, and the alternating pieced blocks create an interesting design. The Nine Patch Variation blocks offer the opportunity to sample just a bit of machine strip piecing. Even if you prefer to hand piece your quilting projects, you might want to try machine piecing this one!

Project Information at a Glance		
Finished Quilt Size:	36½" x 36½"	
Name of Block:	Nine Patch Variation	Twin Star
Finished Block Size:	9" x 9"	9" x 9"
Patchwork Grid:	Nine patch	Nine patch
Number of Blocks to Make:	4	5
Finished Border Width:	4½"	

Materials: 44"-wide fabric

1 yd. large-scale black print (includes border and binding)
⅝ yd. gray print
¼ yd. small-scale black print
¼ yd. plum print
1½ yds. for backing (includes 12" for sleeve)
40" x 40" square of batting

 Large-scale black print

 Gray print

 Small-scale black print

 Plum print

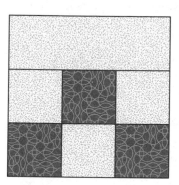

Nine Patch Variation Block
Make 4.

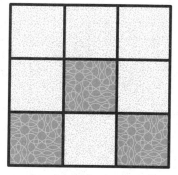

Nine-patch grid

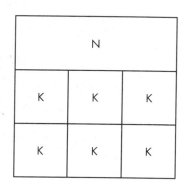

Letters identify templates
and rotary-cut pieces.

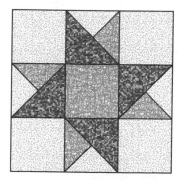

Twin Star Block
Make 5.

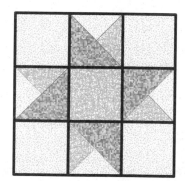

Nine-patch grid

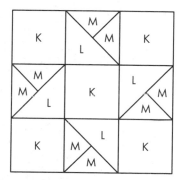

Letters identify templates
and rotary-cut pieces.

Cutting

Setting Pieces				
Cut strips from selvage to selvage across the width of the fabric.				
FABRIC	NO. OF PIECES	SIZE TO MARK	SIZE TO CUT	PLACEMENT
Large-scale black	2	4½" x 36"	5" x 36½"	side borders
	2	4½" x 27"	5" x 27½"	top/bottom borders

Block Pieces to Mark and Cut		
Make templates K, L, M, and N (pages 212–13). *Don't forget to add ¼"-wide seam allowances when cutting pieces.*		
FABRIC	NO. OF PIECES	TEMPLATE
Large-scale black	12	K
Gray	32	K
	20	M
	4	N
Small-scale black	20	L
Plum	5	K
	20	M

Cutting

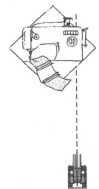

Setting Pieces			
Cut strips from selvage to selvage across the width of the fabric.			
FABRIC	NO. OF PIECES	SIZE TO ROTARY CUT	PLACEMENT
Large-scale black	2	5" x 36½"	side borders
	2	5" x 27½"	top/bottom borders

Block Pieces to Rotary Cut

Cut strips from selvage to selvage across the width of the fabric.

FABRIC	NO. OF PIECES	1ST CUT	2ND CUT	YIELD	PLACEMENT
Large-scale black	1	3½" x 42"			K in strip units
Gray	20	3½" x 3½"			K
	1	3½" x 42"			K in strip units
	5	4¼" x 4¼"	⊠	20	M
	4	3½" x 9½"			N
Small-scale black	10	3⅞" x 3⅞"	◲	20	L
Plum	5	3½" x 3½"			K
	5	4¼" x 4¼"	⊠	20	M

⊠ Cut the squares twice diagonally.
◲ Cut the squares once diagonally.

Block Assembly

Nine Patch Variation Blocks

The following directions are for making 1 Nine Patch Variation block. You can make 1 block at a time or all 4 blocks in assembly-line fashion.

1. Join a gray square (K) and a large-scale black print square (K).

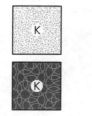 

Make 3.

2. Join the 3 units from step 1 as shown to make a checkerboard section.

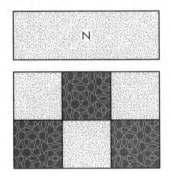

3. Sew a gray rectangle (N) to the checkerboard section to complete the block.

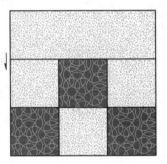

Hooray!

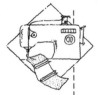

Block Assembly

Nine Patch Variation Blocks

The following directions are for strip piecing all 4 Nine Patch Variation blocks. This block is a good introduction to rotary cutting and strip piecing fabric to create patchwork.

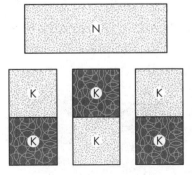

1. Join the 3½" x 42" large-scale black print strip and the 3½" x 42" gray strip on the long side. Using your ruler and rotary cutter, make a clean cut at the end of the strip. Cut 12 units, each 3½" wide, from the strip. If you can't get 12 units from the strip, just cut 2 more 3½"-wide strips long enough to accommodate the needed unit(s).

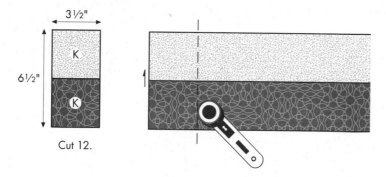

Cut 12.

2. Join 3 units as shown to make a checkerboard section. (See how those seam allowances lock into place?)

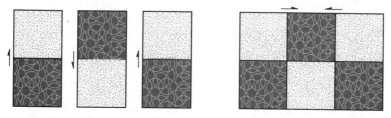

Make 4.

3. Sew a gray print rectangle (N) to the checkerboard section to complete the block.

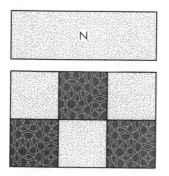

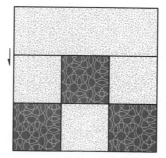

Hooray!

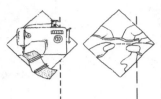

Block Assembly
Twin Star Blocks

The following directions are for making 1 Twin Star Block. Make 1 block at a time or all 5 in assembly-line fashion.

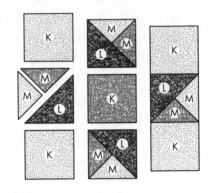

1. Join a gray triangle (M) and a plum triangle (M).

Make 4.

2. Join a small-scale black print triangle (L) and a unit from step 1.

Make 4.

3. Join 2 gray squares (K) and a unit from step 2 to make a row.

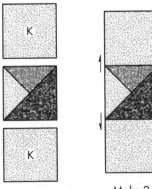

Make 2.

4. Join the remaining 2 units from step 2 and a plum square (K) to make the center row.

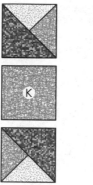 

Make 1.

5. Join the rows to complete 1 block.

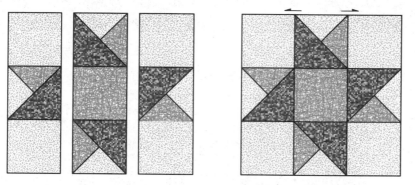

Hooray!

Quilt Top Assembly

1. Arrange the blocks as shown.

2. Sew the blocks together to make 3 rows. Join the rows to create the center patchwork section.

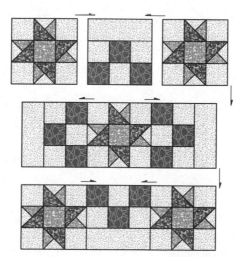

3. Sew border strips to the the top and bottom of the center patchwork section first, then to the sides to complete the quilt top.

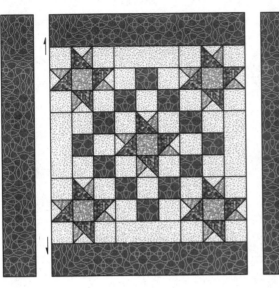

4. Refer to pages 175–208 for directions on finishing your quilt. The quilting design for this quilt is on page 220.

Quilting Suggestion

Ribbons

Here's another choice for a first quilt that is suitable for either hand or machine piecing. Although the quilt has an intricate woven appearance, the same block design and fabric placement are used throughout the quilt. After you've made the same block nine times, you will be really good at it!

Project Information at a Glance

Finished Quilt Size:	39½" x 39½"
Name of Block:	Ribbon Quilt
Finished Block Size:	9" x 9"
Patchwork Grid:	Nine patch
Number of Blocks to Make:	9
Finished Border Widths:	1½" (inner border)
	4½" (outer border)
Finished Corner Squares:	6" x 6"

Navy blue print

 Blue print #1

Blue print #2

Blue print #3

Yellow print

1 yd. navy blue print (includes outer border and binding)

⅛ yd. blue print #1

½ yd. blue print #2 (includes corner squares)

⅜ yd. blue print #3

½ yd. yellow print (includes inner border)

1⅝ yds. for backing (includes 12" for sleeve)

44" x 44" square of batting

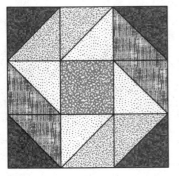

Ribbon Quilt Block
Make 9.

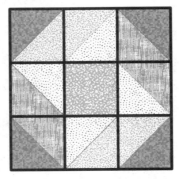

Nine-patch grid

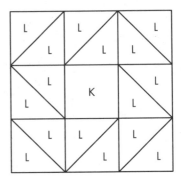

Letters identify templates
and rotary-cut pieces.

Cutting

Setting Pieces				
Cut strips from selvage to selvage across the width of the fabric. *Make template G (page 211).*				
FABRIC	NO. OF PIECES	SIZE TO MARK	SIZE TO CUT	PLACEMENT
Navy blue	4	4½" x 27"	5" x 27½"	outer borders
Yellow	4	1½" x 27"	2" x 27½"	inner borders
Blue #2	4	template G	6½" x 6½"	corner squares

Block Pieces to Mark and Cut

Make templates K and L (page 212).
Don't forget to add ¼"-wide seam allowances when cutting pieces.
Label the blue #2 and blue #3 triangles after you cut them to save time rechecking which blue triangle you need to sew.

FABRIC	NO. OF PIECES	TEMPLATE
Navy blue	36	L
Blue #1	9	K
Blue #2	36	L
Blue #3	36	L
Yellow	36	L

Cutting

Setting Pieces

Cut strips from selvage to selvage across the width of the fabric.

FABRIC	NO. OF PIECES	SIZE TO ROTARY CUT	PLACEMENT
Navy blue	4	5" x 27½"	outer borders
Yellow	4	2" x 27½"	inner borders
Blue #2	4	6½" x 6½"	corner squares

Block Pieces to Rotary Cut

Label the blue #2 and blue #3 triangles after you cut them to save time rechecking which blue triangle you need to sew.

FABRIC	NO. OF PIECES	1ST CUT	2ND CUT	YIELD	PLACEMENT
Navy blue	18	3⅞" x 3⅞"	◪	36	L
Blue #1	9	3½" x 3½"			K
Blue #2	18	3⅞" x 3⅞"	◪	36	L
Blue #3	18	3⅞" x 3⅞"	◪	36	L
Yellow	18	3⅞" x 3⅞"	◪	36	L

◪ Cut the squares once diagonally.

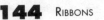

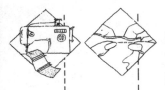

Block Assembly

The following directions are for making 1 Ribbon Quilt block. You can make 1 block at a time or all 9 blocks in assembly-line fashion.

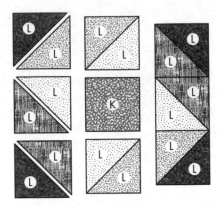

1. Join a navy blue triangle (L) and a blue print #3 triangle (L).

Make 2.

2. Join a blue print #3 triangle (L) and a yellow triangle (L).

Make 2.

3. Join a navy blue triangle (L) and a blue print #2 triangle (L).

Make 2.

4. Join a yellow triangle (L) and a blue print #2 triangle (L).

Make 2.

5. Join a unit from steps 1, 3, and 4 as shown. For row 1, press the seam allowances down. For row 3, turn the unit end to end and press the seam allowances down.

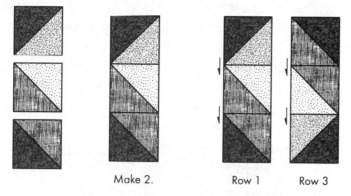

Make 2.   Row 1   Row 3

6. Join 2 units from step 2 and a blue print #1 square (K) as shown to make row 2 of the block.

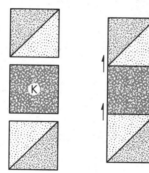

Row 2

7. Join the rows to complete the block.

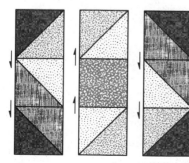
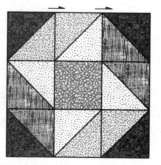

Hooray!

Quilt Top Assembly

1. Since placing seam allowances in opposite directions will make constructing the rows easier, arrange the 9 blocks, 3 across and 3 down, with the seam allowances on the side of the blocks going down, and the seam allowances across the top and bottom of the block going to the right.

2. Rotate the middle block in the first row so the top of the block is on the bottom. Do the same for the first and third blocks in the middle row. Make the last row like the first row. Presto, now your seam allowances will lock into place when you sew your blocks together!

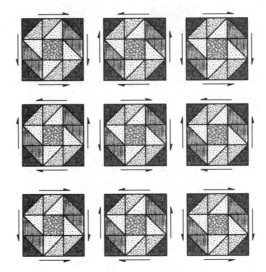

3. Join the blocks into 3 rows. Join the rows to make the center patchwork section.

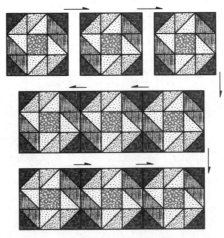

4. Join the 4 inner borders to the 4 outer borders along the long sides.

Make 4.

5. Join pieced border units to the sides of the center patchwork section first. Add a corner square to each end of the 2 remaining pieced border units and sew these to the top and bottom to complete the quilt top.

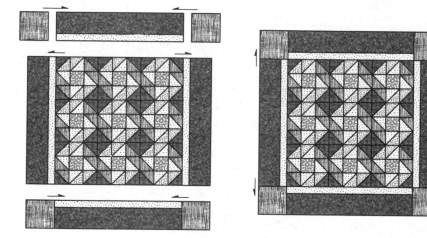

6. Refer to pages 175–208 for directions on finishing your quilt. The quilting design for this quilt is on page 219.

Quilting Suggestion

Simple Stars

If my own mother asked me to teach her how to make a quilt, I might suggest this one. Although the Sawtooth Star block and Plain block (also known as Puss in the Corner) have just a few pieces, they offer the opportunity to use squares, half-square triangles, and quarter-square triangles. The Plain block also gives you the chance to see how easy it is to strip-piece patchwork blocks by machine.

Project Information at a Glance

Finished Quilt Size:	40½" x 40½"	
Name of Block:	Sawtooth Star	Plain
Finished Block Size:	10" x 10"	10" x 10"
Patchwork Grids:	Four patch	Four patch
Number of Blocks to Make:	4	5
Finished Border Width:	5"	
Finished Corner Squares:	5" x 5"	

Materials: 44"-wide fabric

¾ yd. white print
½ yd. beige print
½ yd. dark green print (includes corner squares)
1 yd. pink print (includes border and binding)
1⅝ yds. for backing (includes 12" for sleeve)
44" x 44" square of batting

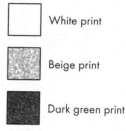

White print

Beige print

Dark green print

Pink print

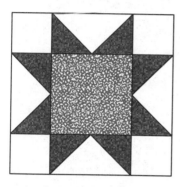

Sawtooth Star Block
Make 4.

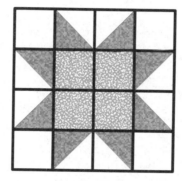

Four-patch grid

O S R S O
S S
S S
R Q R
S S
O S R S O

Letters identify templates
and rotary-cut pieces.

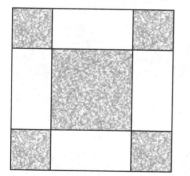

Plain Block
Make 5.

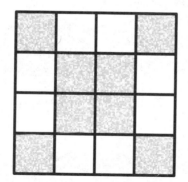

Four-patch grid

O P O
P Q P
O P O

Letters identify templates
and rotary-cut pieces.

Cutting

Setting Pieces				
Make template Q (page 214). *Cut strips from selvage to selvage across the width of the fabric.*				
FABRIC	NO. OF PIECES	SIZE TO MARK	SIZE TO CUT	PLACEMENT
Dark green	4	template Q	5½" x 5½"	corner squares
Pink	4	5" x 30"	5½" x 30½"	borders

Block Pieces to Mark and Cut		
Make templates 0, P, R and S (pages 213–15). *Don't forget to add ¼"-wide seam allowances when cutting pieces.*		
FABRIC	NO. OF PIECES	TEMPLATE
White	20	P
	16	O
	16	R
Beige	5	Q
	20	O
Dark green	32	S
Pink	4	Q

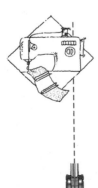

Cutting

Setting Pieces			
Cut strips from selvage to selvage across the width of the fabric.			
FABRIC	NO. OF PIECES	SIZE TO ROTARY CUT	PLACEMENT
Dark green	4	5½" x 5½"	corner squares
Pink	4	5½" x 30½"	borders

FABRIC	NO. OF PIECES	1ST CUT	2ND CUT	YIELD	PLACEMENT
Block Pieces to Rotary Cut					
Cut strips from selvage to selvage across the width of the fabric.					
White	1	5½" x 32"			P in strip unit
	2	3" x 30"			P in strip unit
	16	3" x 3"			O
	4	6¼" x 6¼"	⊠	16	R
Beige	2	3" x 32"			O in strip unit
	1	5½" x 30"			Q in strip unit
Dark green	16	3⅜" x 3⅜"	☒	32	S
Pink	4	5½" x 5½"			Q

⊠ Cut the squares twice diagonally.
☒ Cut the squares once diagonally.

Block Assembly

Sawtooth Star Blocks

The following directions are for making 1 Sawtooth Star block. You can make 1 block at a time or all 4 blocks in assembly-line fashion.

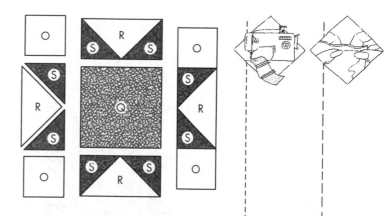

1. Join 2 dark green triangles (S) and 1 white triangle (R) as shown. Refer to page 88 to align these pieces for machine piecing.

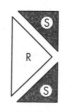

Make 4.

2. Join 2 white squares (O) and a unit from step 1 to make a row.

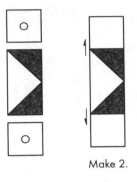

Make 2.

3. Join 2 units from step 1 and 1 pink square (Q) to make the center row.

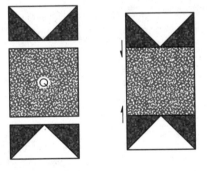

4. Join the rows to complete the block.

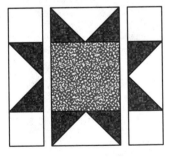
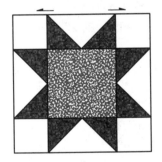

Hooray!

Block Assembly

Plain Blocks

The following directions are for making 1 Plain block. You can make 1 block at a time or all 5 blocks in assembly-line fashion.

1. Join 2 beige squares (O) and 1 white rectangle (P) to make a row.

Make 2.

2. Join 2 white rectangles (P) and 1 beige square (Q) to make the center row.

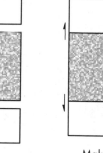

Make 1.

3. Join the rows to complete the block. Was that easy or what?

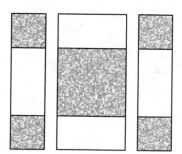
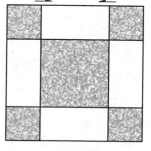

Hooray!

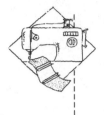

Block Assembly
Plain Blocks

The following directions are for making all 5 Plain blocks, using the strip-piecing method.

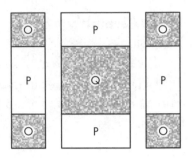

1. Join a 3" x 32" beige strip to each long side of the white 5½" x 32" strip. Use your ruler and rotary cutter to clean-cut the end of the strip set, then cut 10 units, each 3" wide.

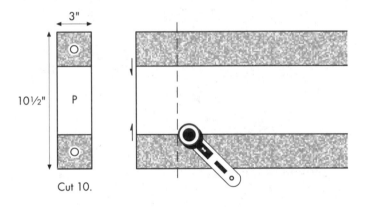

Cut 10.

2. Join a 3" x 30" white strip to each long side of a beige 5½" x 30" strip. Use your ruler and rotary cutter to clean-cut the end of the strip set, then cut 5 units, each 5½" wide.

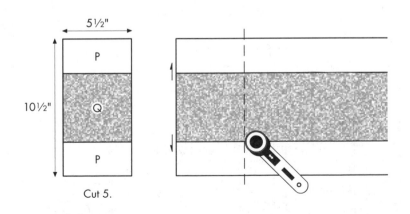

Cut 5.

3. Join 2 units from step 1 and 1 unit from step 2 to complete the block.

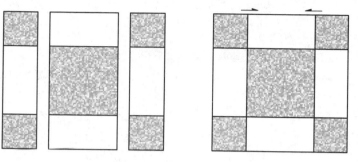

Hooray!

Quilt Top Assembly

1. Arrange the blocks as shown.

2. Join the blocks into 3 rows. Join the rows to make the center patchwork section.

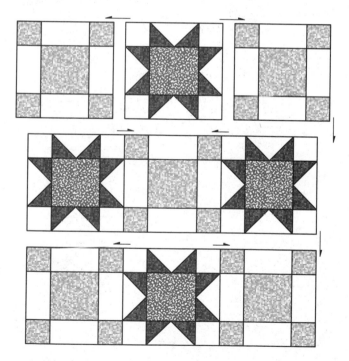

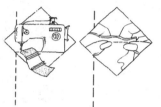

3. Sew border strips to the sides of the center patchwork section first. Add a corner square to each end of the 2 remaining border strips and sew these to the top and bottom to complete the quilt top.

4. Refer to pages 175–208 for directions on finishing your quilt. The quilting designs for this quilt are on pages 218–20.

Quilting Suggestion

Single Irish Chain

What can I say? It doesn't get any easier than this quilt. The Nine Patch blocks can be easily hand pieced or machine strip-pieced, and there are no bias edges at all in this quilt! It would be a great candidate for a graphic statement on a wall or the perfect cuddle quilt for a baby.

Project Information at a Glance

Finished Quilt Size:	36½" x 48½"
Name of Block:	Nine Patch
Finished Block Size:	6" x 6"
Patchwork Grid:	Nine patch
Number of Blocks to Make:	18
Finished Border Width:	3"
Finished Corner Squares:	3" x 3"

Large-scale print

Pink print

Green print

Materials: 44"-wide fabric

1 ¼ yds. large-scale print

¾ yd. pink print (includes corner squares)

1 ¼ yds. green print for border (includes binding)

1 ⅞ yds. for backing (includes 12" for sleeve)

40" x 52" piece of batting

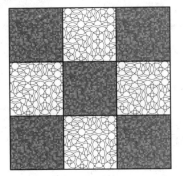

Nine Patch Block
Make 18.

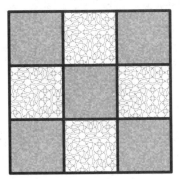

Nine-patch grid

A	A	A
A	A	A
A	A	A

Letters identify templates
and rotary-cut pieces.

Cutting

Setting Pieces

Make templates G and K (pages 211–12).
Cut strips from selvage to selvage across the width of the fabric.

FABRIC	NO. OF PIECES	SIZE TO MARK	SIZE TO CUT	PLACEMENT
Large-scale print	17	template G	6½" x 6½"	setting squares
Pink	4	template K	3½" x 3½"	corner squares
Green	2	3" x 42"	3½" x 42½"	side borders*
	2	3" x 30"	3½" x 30½"	top/bottom borders

*Cut these first. You may be able to cut these across the width of the fabric. If not, cut them from the length of the fabric.

Block Pieces to Mark and Cut

Make template A (page 210).
Don't forget to add ¼"-wide seam allowances when cutting pieces.

FABRIC	NO. OF PIECES	TEMPLATE
Large-scale print	72	A
Pink	90	A

Cutting

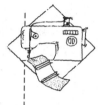

Setting Pieces

Cut strips from selvage to selvage across the width of the fabric.

FABRIC	NO. OF PIECES	SIZE TO ROTARY CUT	PLACEMENT
Large-scale print	17	6½" x 6½"	setting squares
Pink	4	3½" x 3½"	corner squares
Green	2	3½" x 42½"	side borders*
	2	3½" x 30½"	top/bottom borders

*Cut these first. You may be able to cut these across the width of the fabric. If not, cut them from the length of the fabric.

Block Pieces to Rotary Cut

Cut strips from selvage to selvage across the width of the fabric.

FABRIC	NO. OF PIECES	SIZE TO ROTARY CUT
Large-scale print	4	2½" x 42"
	2	2½" x 7"
	1	2½" x 12"
Pink	5	2½" x 42"
	1	2½" x 7"
	2	2½" x 12"

Block Assembly

The following directions are for making 1 Nine Patch block. You can make 1 block at a time or all 18 blocks in assembly-line fashion.

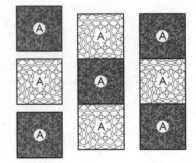

1. Join 2 pink squares (A) and 1 large-scale print square (A) as shown to make a row.

Make 2.

2. Join 2 large-scale print squares (A) and 1 pink square (A) as shown to make a center row.

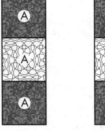

Make 1.

3. Join the rows to complete the block.

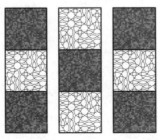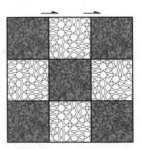

Hooray!

Block Assembly

The following directions are for making all 18 Nine Patch blocks using the strip-piecing method.

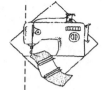

1. Sew a 2½"-wide pink strip to each long side of a 2½"-wide large-scale print strip. Make 1 more identical strip set. Make a third strip set using the 12"-long pieces. Use a ruler and rotary cutter to clean-cut the edges of the strip sets, then cut a total of 36 units, each 2½" wide.

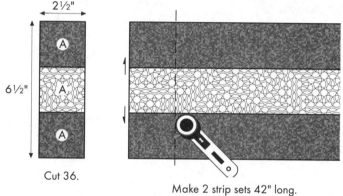

2½"

6½"

Cut 36.

Make 2 strip sets 42" long.
Make 1 strip set 12" long.

2. Sew a 2½"-wide large-scale print strip to each long side of a 2½"-wide pink strip. Make another strip set using the 7"-long pieces. Use a ruler and rotary cutter to clean-cut the edges of the strip sets, then cut a total of 18 units, each 2½" wide.

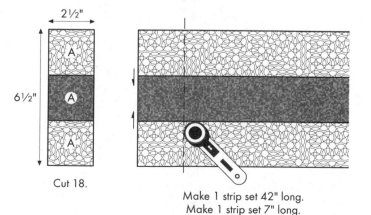

2½"

6½"

Cut 18.

Make 1 strip set 42" long.
Make 1 strip set 7" long.

3. Join 2 units from step 1 and 1 unit from step 2 to complete a block.

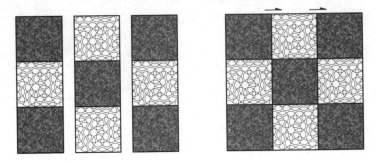

Hooray!

Quilt Top Assembly

1. Arrange the Nine Patch blocks and the alternating large-scale print squares as shown.

2. Join the blocks into 7 rows. Join the rows to make the center patchwork section.

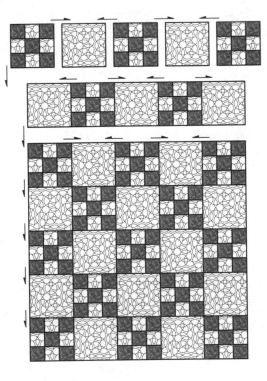

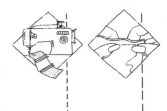

3. Sew border strips to the sides of the center patchwork section first. Add a corner square to each end of the 2 remaining border strips and sew these to the top and bottom to complete the quilt top.

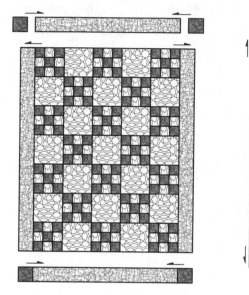

4. Refer to pages 175–208 for directions on finishing your quilt. The quilting designs for this quilt are on page 217. The border design below will be easier to mark than the random vine design shown on page 96.

Quilting Suggestion

Home Sweet Home

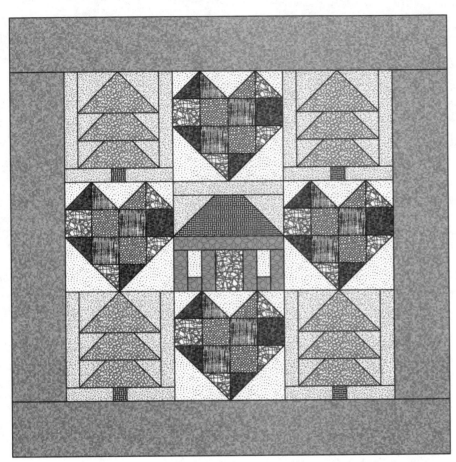

This is not a difficult quilt to make, but it does have three different block designs, which will give you more to think about! If you just approach each block design one at a time, you'll be fine. If you are machine piecing this quilt, you will learn how to make machine templates and how to cut fabric pieces with the template attached to a ruler (see pages 81–82).

Project Information at a Glance			
Finished Quilt Size:	32½" x 32½"		
Name of Block:	Tree	Heart	House
Finished Block Size:	8" x 8"	8" x 8"	8" x 8"
Patchwork Grids:	Four patch	Four patch	Four patch
Number of Blocks to Make:	4	4	1
Finished Border Width:	4"		

Materials: 44"-wide fabric

⅛ yd. red print #1
⅛ yd. red print #2
⅛ yd. red print #3
⅛ yd. red print #4
¼ yd. light beige print
⅛ yd. medium beige print
⅜ yd. light blue print
⅜ yd. green print
⅛ yd. black print
⅞ yd. medium blue print (includes border and binding)
1½ yds. for backing (includes 12" for sleeve)
36" x 36" square of batting

 Red print #1

 Red print #2

 Red print #3

 Red print #4

Light beige print

 Medium beige print

Light blue print

Green print

Black print

Medium blue print

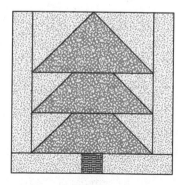

Tree Block
Make 4.

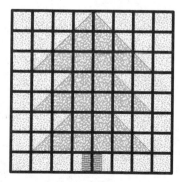

Four-patch grid

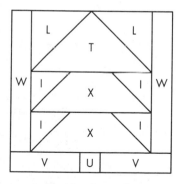

Letters identify templates
and rotary-cut pieces.

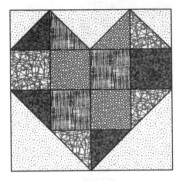

Heart Block
Make 4.

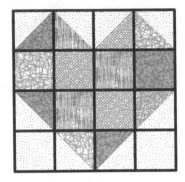

Four-patch grid

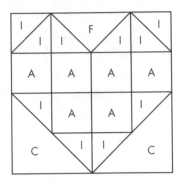

Letters identify templates
and rotary-cut pieces.

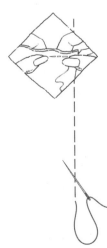

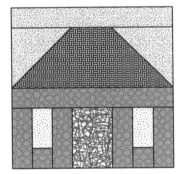

House Block
Make 1.

Four-patch grid

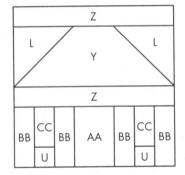

Letters identify templates
and rotary-cut pieces.

Cutting

Setting Pieces				
Cut strips from selvage to selvage across the width of the fabric.				
FABRIC	NO. OF PIECES	SIZE TO MARK	SIZE TO CUT	PLACEMENT
Medium blue	2	4" x 24"	4½" x 24½"	side borders
	2	4" x 32"	4½" x 32½"	top/bottom borders

Block Pieces to Mark and Cut

Make templates A, C, I, F, L, T, U, V, W, X, Y, Z, AA, BB, and CC (pages 210–16).

Don't forget to add ¼"-wide seam allowances when cutting pieces. Since you have a lot of pieces to cut, I suggest you label the pieces as you cut them so you will have a quick reference.

FABRIC	NO. OF PIECES	TEMPLATE	FABRIC	NO. OF PIECES	TEMPLATE
Red #1	4	A	Medium beige	1	Z
	12	I		2	U
Red #2	8	A		4	BB
	4	I	Light blue	10	L
Red #3	8	A		16	I
	4	I		1	Z
Red #4	4	A		8	W
	12	I		8	V
	1	AA	Green	4	T
Light beige	8	C		8	X*
	8	I	Black	4	U
	4	F		1	Y*
	2	CC			

*Cut out templates X and Y on the inner sewing line.

Cutting

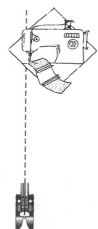

Setting Pieces			
Cut strips from selvage to selvage across the width of the fabric.			
FABRIC	NO. OF PIECES	SIZE TO ROTARY CUT	PLACEMENT
Medium blue	2	4½" x 24½"	side borders
	2	4½" x 32½"	top/bottom borders

Block Pieces to Rotary Cut

Since you have lots of pieces to cut, I suggest you label the pieces as you cut them, so you will have a quick reference.

FABRIC	NO. OF PIECES	1ST CUT	2ND CUT	YIELD	PLACEMENT
Red #1	4	2½" x 2½"			A
	6	2⅞" x 2⅞"	◪	12	I (Heart block)
Red #2	8	2½" x 2½"			A
	2	2⅞" x 2⅞"	◪	4	I (Heart block)
Red #3	8	2½" x 2½"			A
	2	2⅞" x 2⅞"	◪	4	I (Heart block)
Red #4	4	2½" x 2½"			A
	6	2⅞" x 2⅞"	◪	12	I (Heart block)
	1	2½" x 3½"			AA
Light beige	4	4⅞" x 4⅞"	◪	8	C
	4	2⅞" x 2⅞"	◪	8	I (Heart block)
	1	5¼" x 5¼"	⊠	4	F
	2	1½" x 2½"			CC
Medium beige	1	1½" x 8½"			Z
	2	1½" x 1½"			U (House block)
	4	1½" x 3½"			BB
Light blue	5	3⅞" x 3⅞"	◪	10	L
	8	2⅞" x 2⅞"	◪	16	I (Tree block)
	1	1½" x 8½"			Z
	8	1½" x 7½"			W
	8	1½" x 4"			V
Green	1	7¼" x 7¼"	⊠	4	T
	8	machine template X*			X
Black	4	1½" x 1½"			U (Tree block)
	1	machine template Y*			Y

Make machine templates X and Y (with ¼"-wide seam allowances included as described on page 81).

⊠ Cut the squares twice diagonally.
◪ Cut the squares once diagonally.

Block Assembly
Tree Blocks

The following directions are for making 1 Tree Block. You can make 1 block at a time or all 4 blocks in assembly-line fashion.

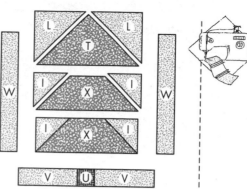

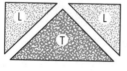 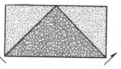

1. Join 2 light blue triangles (L) and 1 green triangle (T).

Make 1.

2. Join 2 light blue triangles (I) and 1 green trapezoid (X).

Make 2.

3. Join the unit from step 1 and the units from step 2 as shown.

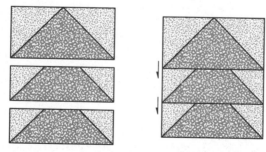

4. Sew the light blue rectangles (W) to each side of the unit from step 3.

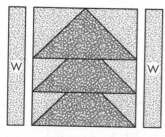 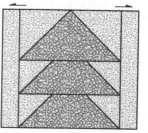

5. Join the light blue rectangles (V) and the black square (U).

Make 1.

6. Sew the unit from step 5 to the bottom of the unit from step 4 to complete the block.

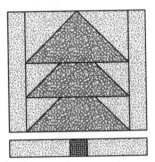

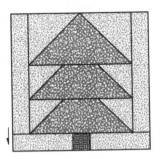

Hooray!

Heart Blocks

The following directions are for making 1 Heart block. You can make 1 block at a time or all 4 blocks in assembly-line fashion.

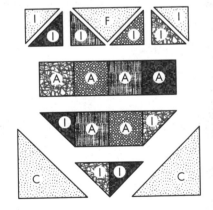

1. Join a light beige triangle (I) and a red print #1 triangle (I). Join a light beige triangle (I) and a red print #4 triangle (I).

Make 1.   Make 1.

2. Sew a red print #2 triangle (I) and a red print #3 triangle (I) to a light beige triangle (F) as shown.

Make 1.

3. Join the units from steps 1 and 2 as shown to make row 1.

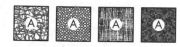 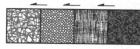

Row 1

4. Join the red print #1, #2, #3, and #4 squares (A) to make row 2.

 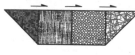

Row 2

5. Join a red print #1 triangle (I), a red print #2 square (A), a red print #3 square (A), and a red print #4 triangle (I) to make row 3.

Row 3

6. Join a red print #4 triangle (I) and a red print #1 triangle (I) to make row 4.

Row 4

7. Join rows 1, 2, 3, and 4.

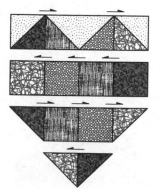 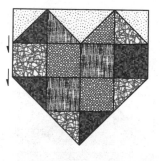

8. Sew 2 light beige triangles (C) to the assembled rows as shown to complete the block.

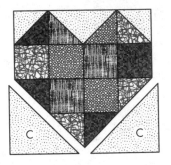
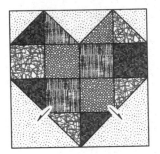

Hooray!

House Block

The following directions are for making 1 House block.

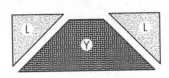

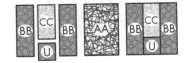

1. Join 2 light blue triangles (L) and a black trapezoid (Y).

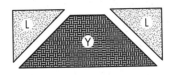
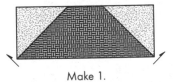

Make 1.

2. Sew the light blue rectangle (Z) and the medium beige rectangle (Z) to the unit from step 1 as shown.

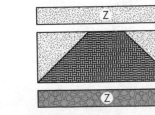
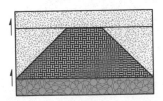

3. Join a light beige rectangle (CC) and a medium beige square (U).

Make 2.

4. Sew a medium beige rectangle (BB) to each side of a unit from step 3.

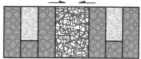

Make 2.

5. Sew a unit from step 4 to each side of the red print #4 rectangle (AA).

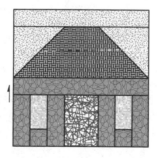

6. Join the unit from step 5 and the unit from step 2 to complete the block.

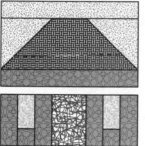

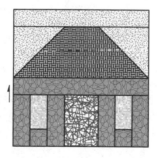

Hooray!

Quilt Top Assembly

1. Arrange the patchwork blocks as shown.
2. Join the blocks into 3 rows. Join the rows to make the center patchwork section.

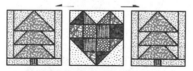

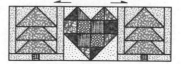

3. Sew border strips to the sides of the center patchwork section first, then to the top and bottom to complete the quilt top.

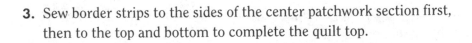

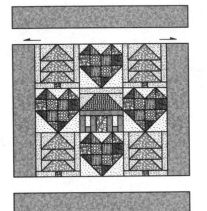 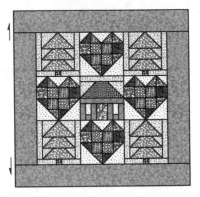

4. Refer to pages 175–208 for directions on finishing your quilt.

Quilting Suggestion

The Quilting Process

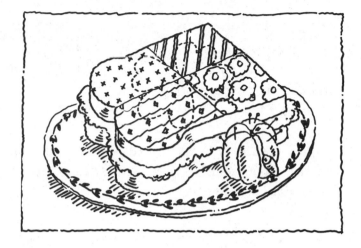

Whew! You are now ready to sandwich and baste your quilt. The sandwich consists of the backing (the back of the quilt), the batting (the filler in the middle), and the patchwork top.

Selecting Quilting Designs

If you think most quilters are so talented that they draw those pretty designs on their quilts freehand, let me dispel that thought right now. We are good, but most of us aren't that good! Quilting stencils are available in a variety of sizes and shapes for block and border designs.

The stencils are placed on the quilt top, and the designs are marked either before or after basting the quilt. Remember, you don't want the markings to show after quilting, so be careful about the type of marking instrument you use. Mark a scrap piece of your fabrics to test the removal of any marking instrument before marking your quilt top; then mark only as dark as you need to, to see the lines. See "Fabric Marking Instruments" on pages 33–34.

You will notice little spaces between the lines of the stencils. These are called hedges and are used to keep the stencil intact. Even though you don't draw a line there, you do quilt through that area.

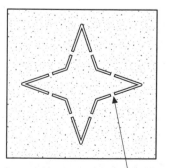

These spaces in the stencil are called hedges.

Since marking the quilting designs is not one of my favorite quilting tasks, I prefer to mark small segments of the quilt top at a time. Marking just before I quilt also means the markings are fresh and easier to see.

Sometimes you can avoid marking quilting lines by following the print of the fabric when you quilt. For example, you can quilt the lines of a striped fabric without marking them.

Curved-Line Options

Purchased stencils can be used to create curved-line designs, or you can trace around simple shapes such as hearts, circles, and ovals to make curved-lined designs.

You can buy quilt stencils . . .

OR

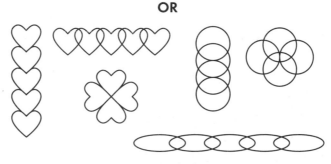

. . . trace simple shapes.

When considering what type of design to quilt, keep in mind that more lines in the design mean more quilting time. In the beginning, you might want to select designs with fewer lines until you are comfortable with your quilting. Below are examples of popular quilting designs, including a feathered heart, feathered circle, and feathered border design.

 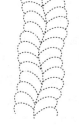 

This first group, although pretty, will take some time to quilt.

This second group is a better choice for a beginner.

It is always faster and more efficient to continue a line of quilting without stopping one place and starting another. A continuous line is helpful when hand quilting, but even more important when machine quilting. If the quilting lines in the design are connected, you can easily quilt without stopping and starting. The following illustration shows how individual designs can be connected to create continuous-line designs.

Continuous-Line Options

These designs mean stopping and starting.

These designs are continuous.

Straight-Line Options

You can quilt in-the-ditch, which means to stitch right next to the down side of the seam (the side of the seam without seam allowances). This is a common choice when machine quilting.

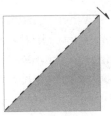

Quilting in-the-ditch

If you are hand quilting, I suggest you quilt ¼" from the seam lines so you don't have to consider the seam allowances. This is called outline quilting. You can eyeball the ¼", or mark the line by placing your ¼" ruler line on the seam and marking along the edge. The Hera fabric marker can also be used to mark straight lines if your fabric isn't too busy (see page 34).

Outline quilting

Quilting parallel straight lines at a 45° angle is another good choice for beginners. Actually, quilting at this angle is the easiest direction to quilt because the fabric has the greatest amount of stretch along the bias. To mark parallel 45° lines, place the 45° line on your ruler on any straight edge. To mark the lines a set distance apart, align the previous marking with the desired width on the ruler.

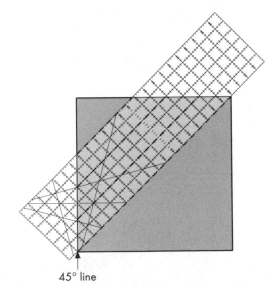

45° line

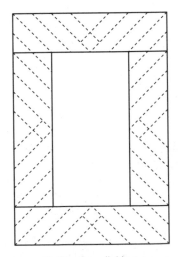

Quilting parallel lines

Cross-hatching produces a nice texture and is achieved by quilting two sets of 45° lines.

Cross-hatching

Straight lines can be used creatively on the patchwork or to emphasize a particular aspect of the design.

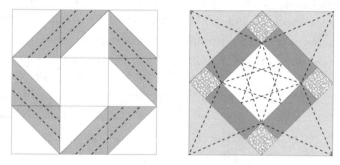

Creative use of straight lines

If you are going to machine quilt your project, keep in mind that the goal is to avoid stopping and starting often. In the beginning, straight lines will be easiest to quilt because you will have the advantage of the feed dogs pulling your project along at a regular rate (see page 197). Curved designs are worked in a freehand motion as you move the project along the design (see page 197). This is an acquired skill, and you will do best with continuous designs. Make a trial sandwich of batting and scrap fabric and practice free-motion quilting before starting on your quilt. You may want to consider straight-line options for your first few projects until you feel comfortable with free-motion quilting.

Machine-Quilting Considerations

Border Options

Stencils for borders come in a variety of widths. The repeat of the design will also vary. Select a design that is close to the width of your border. Getting it to fit around the corners usually requires a bit of flexibility. Before marking, place the corner of the stencil or pattern on the corner of the border and move it along to see how it will match up. If it is just a little too short or a little too long coming into the next corner, you can extend or shorten the design a bit as you mark it. Trust me, no one will know you did this.

If the design is way off, try starting in the middle of the border with the middle of the design and see how it comes into the corners. Even if you make a whole new corner design, at least it will be the same in all four corners.

Another option is to break up the midpoint of each border with either patchwork or quilting, so the design is not continuous. This means you can mark each corner, and the borders will just meet in the middle of the sides. Or, you can eliminate the continuous corner portion of the border and break it up with a different quilting design in the corner.

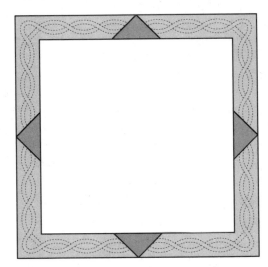

You can break the midpoint
of the border with patchwork.

You can break the midpoint of the border
with a different quilting design.

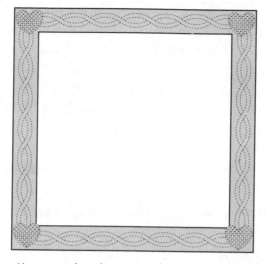

You can replace the corners of the border design
with a different quilting design.

For your convenience, quilting designs are provided on pages 217–20 for the Simple Stars, Star Bright, Ribbons, and Single Irish Chain quilts. You have a couple of options for using the designs to mark your quilt top.

- Trace the shapes onto plastic template material and cut them out; then place the shapes on your quilt top and draw around them.
- Trace the designs onto the uncoated side of freezer paper and cut them out; then place the shapes on your quilt top, pressing lightly to hold them in place, and trace around them. If you are going to machine quilt, you have the option of leaving the freezer paper in place and quilting around the edge of the paper. You can use the same shape several times before the stickiness is gone.

Choosing the Batting

Many types of quilt batting are available in a variety of lofts (how thick the batting is), fiber content, and even color. Polyester battings come in low-loft, traditional loft, and extra-loft. If you are hand quilting your project, I suggest you choose a low-loft bonded polyester batting. Bonding is a coating applied to the batting so the fibers will not work their way through the top of the quilt. When batting migrates through the top of the quilt, it is called "bearding."

Polyester battings are available in white for light quilts, and black or charcoal for dark quilts. The suggested quilting distance for most polyester battings is every 3" to 4". This means no more than a 4" area should be left unquilted. There are also some polyester quilt battings designed just for fluffy tied quilts.

Cotton battings are also available in a variety of lofts, but they vary in the amount of quilting required. Some cotton battings require quilting as close as every ¼" to ½". If you don't quilt that close, the cotton batting could pull apart. Other cotton battings suggest up to a 10" quilting distance. The required quilting distance for each type of cotton batting depends on how it was manufactured.

Cotton batting is often the choice of the machine quilter because it will "grab hold" of the cotton fabric in the quilt and help keep the layers together during the quilting process. Some manufacturers suggest you prewash their battings before quilting. When you wash batting, soak and spin only in the machine, never agitate. Some cotton battings are designed just for machine quilting.

Wool batting is now available. It is low-loft and easy to hand quilt, but it is a bit more costly.

- If you are going to hand quilt your first project, use a polyester batting. Polyester battings are easier to needle than cotton.
- If you want to machine quilt your first project, consider a cotton batting with a 6" to 10" quilting requirement.
- If you are going to tie your quilt, a high-loft polyester batting is a good choice.

Before you purchase batting for your quilt, know its fiber content and the suggested quilting distance. If it is polyester, confirm that it is bonded. If it is cotton, find out if prewashing is necessary or suggested. Read the package directions.

Batting is sold in prepackaged bags or is cut from a large roll. If your batting was in a bag, take it out of the bag and let it relax for a few hours before sandwiching and basting your project. Cut the batting at least 4" larger than your quilt top.

Cut the backing approximately 4" larger than your quilt top. Since all the projects in this book are 40½" wide or less, you will cut the backing from one piece of fabric. You may want to choose a print fabric for your backing so your beginning quilting stitches will not be so noticeable. See the tip on page 187.

Making the Backing

Seam a Backing (if your fabric isn't wide enough)

When your project width plus the extra 4" is wider than the width of one piece of fabric, you will need to seam two lengths of fabric. Remove the selvages from both fabric lengths. Sew the two lengths together with a ¼"-wide center seam, or split one length lengthwise and sew the pieces to both sides of the other length. Press the seam allowances open.

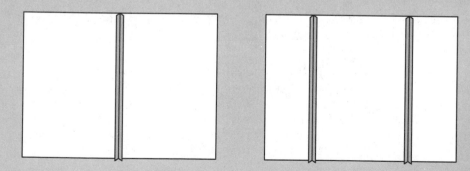

Continued on page 184

If you prefer the two-seam option for your backing, place the two fabric pieces right sides together (with the selvages already removed). Using a ¼"-wide seam allowance, stitch along the length of both sides. Align the seams in the center as shown. Make a small slit at the edge of one fold and tear one length in half. Press the seam allowances open.

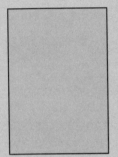 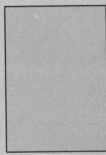

Two lengths with selvages removed

Seamed right
sides together

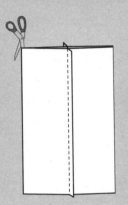

Match seams,
snip, and tear.

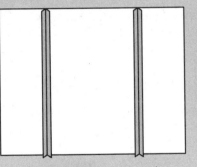

One full length in center with
two partial lengths on each side

If you are working on a small project, basting the three layers together on your own should not be difficult. When you are working on a large project, however, three friends can help make the process so much easier because one person can work from each side of the quilt. You could always bake up a batch of cookies and resort to bribery! Baste with needle and thread for hand quilting. Use safety pins to baste for machine quilting.

Basting: Step by Step

1. Spread the backing, wrong side up, on a clean surface. You can use a table or the floor, depending on the size of your project and whether you are comfortable working at floor level. Use masking tape or pins to anchor the backing, being careful not to stretch it out of shape. If you are working on a table, you can use large binder clamps to anchor the backing.

2. Spread and smooth the quilt batting over the backing, making sure it covers the entire backing.

3. Center the quilt top on the batting, right side up, smoothing out any wrinkles. Make sure the edges of the quilt top are parallel to the edges of the backing.

4. If you are going to *hand quilt*, begin basting in the middle and work to the outside edge. Make vertical and horizontal rows of basting stitches in a grid, about 5" to 8" apart and two diagonal rows from corner to corner. Use a size 7 long, darner needle with light-colored thread.
   If you are going to *machine quilt*, pin-baste with size 1 or 2, rustproof safety pins. Beginning in the middle, place the pins about 4" apart, but leave them open. Once all the pins are in place, close them with a grapefruit spoon or the handy Kwik Klip tool so your fingers don't become sore. The shank of the pin will rest in the groove of the grapefruit spoon or the Kwik Klip, making it easier to close the pins without using your fingers.

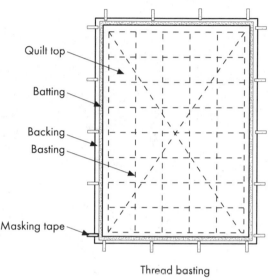

Thread basting

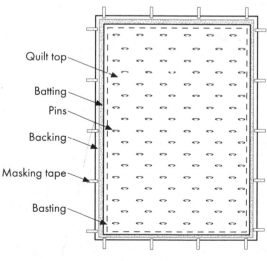

Pin basting

Do not use dark-colored thread to baste a light-colored quilt, because the dye from the thread may transfer to the quilt.

Use a double length of thread and baste in one direction, leaving half the thread to rethread your needle; then baste in the opposite direction. This will eliminate knots.

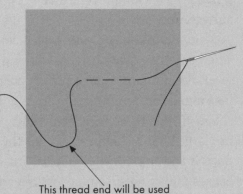

This thread end will be used to baste in the opposite direction.

5. Bring the edge of the backing around to the front of the quilt top and baste in place to contain any exposed batting while quilting. If you leave the batting edges exposed, the fibers will not only dust your house, they will also get on top of the quilt.

Quilting by Hand

If you have chosen to hand quilt your quilt, you'll want to know a little bit about hand-quilting supplies. When it comes to choosing a hoop or frame, you can quilt both large and small projects in a quilting hoop or hand-held frame. The hoop needs to be able to catch the perimeter of the project and still be comfortable to use. If your underneath hand can't reach the center of the hoop, it is too big.

Place the inside portion of your hoop in the middle of your project and slip the top part of the hoop over the fabric. The fabric should be smooth and taut on both the top and bottom. You need to manipulate the fabric as you quilt, so do not pull the fabric as tight as a drum. To loosen the fabric a little, put a bit of pressure in the center of the hoop. Tighten the screws on the hoop. Quilt your project from the center out in a logical vertical, horizontal, and diagonal fashion. Use a size 9 or 10 between needle and quilting thread.

Quilting thread comes in a variety of colors. As a beginner, one way to make your stitches less noticeable is to use a thread that matches the fabric you are quilting. Yes, it is okay to use different-colored quilting threads on the same project. But if you choose this option, select a print fabric for the backing so the different thread colors will not be noticeable on the back.

Thread your quilting needle with a 15" length of cotton or cotton-covered polyester quilting thread. If you are right-handed, thread the needle from the end coming off the spool. If you are left-handed, cut the thread from the spool and thread the end you just cut. Knot the end that did not go through the eye of the needle.

Right-hand threading   Left-hand threading

If you are right-handed and use a thread holder with a magnet, you can thread an entire package of quilting needles onto the spool and place the threaded needles on the magnet. Just pull the needle and the thread length you want each time you need another threaded needle.

Next, you will make a knot.

Take the long end of the thread and lay it alongside the needle. Grab hold of it with the fingers holding the needle.

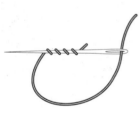

Wrap the thread around the needle 3 or 4 times.

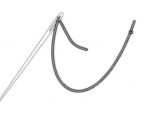

Pull the needle through the thread wraps and slide the wraps to the end of the thread, making the knot.

To bury the knot, insert the needle through the top and batting (but not through the back of the quilt) about 1" from where you will begin quilting. Place your other hand under the quilt to confirm that you have not gone all the way through. Pull the thread through to the knot, then give a tug to pop the knot between the layers. If the knot resists, wrap the thread near the top of the quilt around your finger and try again.

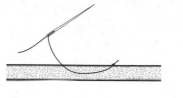 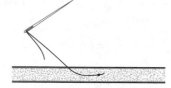

Tug on the thread until the knot
goes between the layers.

Experience Your First Quilting Stitches

Hand quilting is an acquired skill, and your first quilting stitches are probably not something you'll want to write about to Mother. However, the more you quilt, the better your stitches will become. You are striving for neat, even stitches, not tiny stitches! The best way to have great quilting stitches is to quilt—and quilt, and quilt. I strongly suggest that you quilt thirty minutes each day to build up strength in your fingers and to become accustomed to the technique. I make my students take an oath in my quilting classes to do this because it is the best way to learn and enjoy hand quilting. So, please raise your right hand and repeat after me, "I _____(your name) promise to quilt thirty minutes each day."

My favorite way to quilt is the rocker quilting method. In this technique, the needle is rocked back and forth in a continuous motion to make a line of quilting stitches. You can use this stitch to quilt to the side or toward you, using the top of the thimble on your middle finger, or to quilt away from you, using the side of a tailor's thimble or a leather thimble on your thumb.

Being able to quilt in all directions will save you time and reduce the repetitive use of the same fingers. However, if you have never quilted before, do not try to learn both directions at once. Try one or the other and see which seems to fit you better, then pursue it until you are comfortable with it. Once you have mastered one direction, try the other.

Since I used the word "comfortable," let me caution you that your first hand-quilting experiences will feel awkward. It is like learning to ride your two-wheeler bike as a child. You probably fell off several times and thought you would never get the hang of it. Then one day, you were riding. It still wasn't a pretty picture, but you were riding. About two weeks later, you were probably coasting down the hill with no hands, much to your parents dismay! So, just hang in there. Hand quilting can be a relaxing activity, even somewhat mesmerizing, and you will probably enjoy it. Just remember to relax and breathe!

Since placing your finger underneath a quilt and touching it with a needle is a new experience in your life, your finger may become sore. After awhile, your finger will toughen up. Until it does, place a little tab of cloth adhesive tape on the pad of your underneath finger to protect it. Some hand quilters use a thimble on their underneath finger to angle the needle back up to the top, but this dulls the needle. It is also more difficult to get used to because you don't have the sensation of touch to rely upon. Try both methods and choose the one that is most comfortable for you.

Quilt to the Side and Toward You

Place a closed-top thimble on your middle finger. For the sake of clarity, I am going to describe these step-by-step directions for a right-handed quilter. If you are left-handed, the method is identical; you will just be using opposite hands.

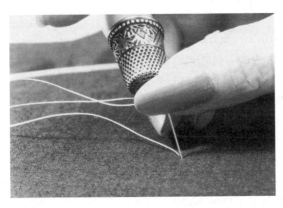

1. Resting the eye of the needle against the top of the thimble, put the needle straight down into the quilt with your right hand.

2. Rest the index finger of your left hand under the quilt in the same area. It is waiting to feel the needle. Remember, you are not going for blood here. You just want to feel the sensation of the point coming through. Once the needle point is

resting on the finger underneath, release your fingers from the needle, supporting the needle eye against the top of the thimble.

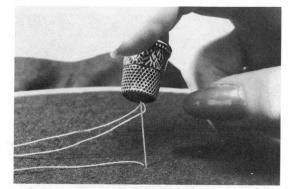

3. With the eye of the needle against the top of the thimble, pivot the needle down, parallel to the top of the quilt. Move the underneath finger back slightly and push up from the bottom of the quilt on the shank of the needle. The thumb on the right hand pushes down in front to create a "hill." In the photo at right, look for the hill being created by the finger pushing up from the bottom along the shank of the needle and the thumb in front.

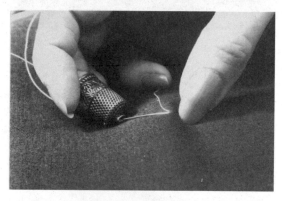

4. Push the needle forward through the hill to make the stitch. OK, breathe! If your first stitch is too long, it is because you are pushing forward before you should. Patience is a virtue.

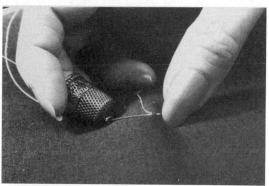

5. Repeat the process by bringing the needle back up again to a vertical position. You will find it is easier this time because the fabric is holding the needle. Push down, just feel the point, pivot the needle parallel to the top, push up on the shank with the finger below, push down in front of the hill with the thumb, and push forward to make the stitch.

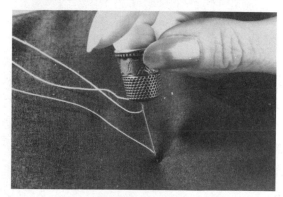

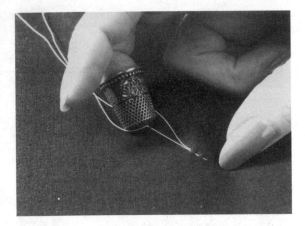

You should now have two stitches on the needle. Look and see if they are close in size. Remember, you are striving for neat and uniform stitches. It is easier to make the adjustments when you are just matching two stitches in size, so I suggest that you pull the thread through and continue to put two more stitches on the needle. When you feel more comfortable and your two stitches are routinely the same size, add a third and then a fourth stitch to your needle before pulling the thread through.

You can save lots of time if you pull the thread through the two stitches just enough to begin two more stitches and then pull the thread all the way through all four stitches.

Quilt Away with a Thumb Thimble

You can use either a leather thimble or a tailor's thimble on your thumb, since only the side of the thimble is used in this method. A tailor's thimble should fit comfortably (not loose enough to spin or so tight that it turns your thumb blue). The top of your thumb should be just about level with the opening in the top. You are going to do exactly the same thing described above, except different fingers are going to accomplish the tasks.

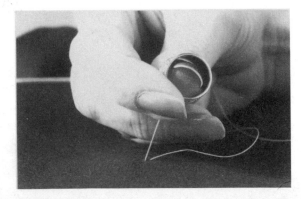

1. Holding the needle between your first and third fingers, rest the eye of the needle against the side of the thimble. Insert the needle into the quilt.

2. As soon as the finger underneath gets the point (sorry, couldn't resist that pun), let go with your fingers and pivot the needle parallel to the top of the quilt with the thimble. Push up along the shank with the underneath finger to create the hill and push down with your index finger in front of the point. Do you see that hill?

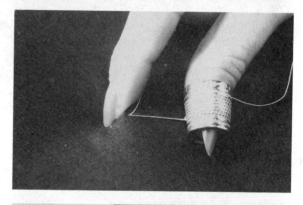

3. Push the needle forward to make the stitch. OK, breathe!

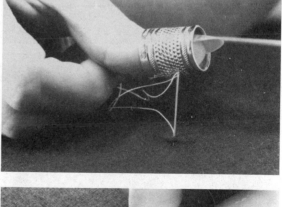

4. Pivot the needle back up to a vertical position, push down through the top, and continue the same motions until you have those two stitches on the needle. Pull the thread through.

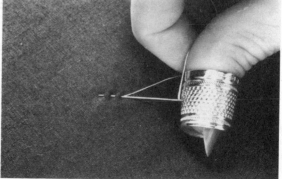

You can eliminate stops and starts by sliding your needle under the quilt top to another location. This traveling tip will come in handy often. I suggest you try it right away!

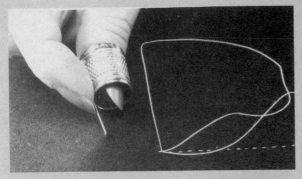

Slip the needle between the layers (place your hand under the quilt to make sure you don't go all the way through). Bring only the point up and grab hold of it. The eye of the needle should still be between the layers.

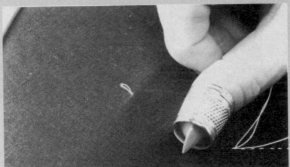

Now turn the eye of the needle around and push it along under the quilt top and up through the fabric where you want to be. Since you will be pushing on the point of the needle to push the eye through, you need to do this with a metal thimble!

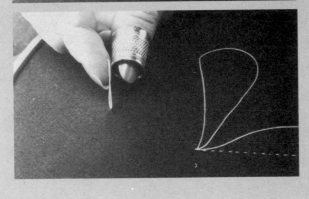

Grab the eye of the needle and pull the thread through. If that wasn't far enough, continue to rotate the needle under the quilt top, grabbing the eye and the point alternately until you have reached your new location.

This quilting technique is not as gruesome as it sounds. It simply means that the needle is pushed down through the top of the quilt with one hand and pulled through by the underneath hand and returned to the top.

Stab Stitch (no ouch!)

The stab stitch is not as widely used as the rocker quilting stitch because, for most people, it is slower, and keeping the stitches straight on the underside takes some practice. However, even if you use the rocker stitch for most of your quilting, you may want to use this method to take one or two stitches when you come to an area where layers of seam allowances make it difficult to rock the needle. Since you are sewing blindly from underneath, push the needle down from the top with your hand that is not your primary hand (top photo) and return it to the top with your primary hand under the quilt (bottom photo). This will give you better control.

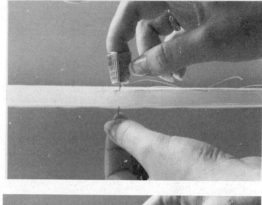

Take the thread that is coming out of the quilt and wrap it around the point of the needle about three or four times. Slip the needle through the wraps and slip the knot to the end of the thread, near the top of the quilt. Put the needle between the layers and "pop" the knot inside the quilt. Cut the thread and let it disappear inside the quilt.

End a Line of Quilting

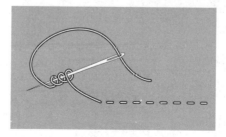

Wrapping thread to make knot

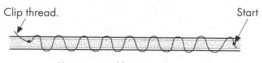

Clip thread.   Start

Knot popped between layers

To avoid having shorter quilting stitches on the back of the quilt than on the front, insert the point of the needle as perpendicular to the quilt top as possible when you take your stitches.

To make straight stitches, bring the needle shank back down on the line of stitches that you have already quilted. This will keep the point straight as it goes into the quilt top.

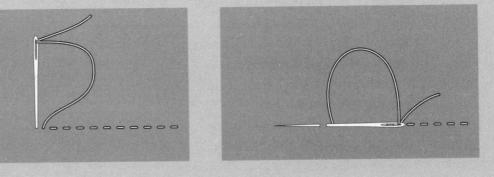

Quilting by Machine

Machine quilting takes less time than hand quilting, but it is also an acquired skill. The more you do it, the more comfortable you'll feel. Many machine quilters listen to music while they quilt to get into a relaxed rhythm.

An even-feed foot or a walking foot is a definite must for machine quilting straight lines or wide curves. It permits the multiple layers to be pulled through the machine at the same rate. You manually turn the quilt to change direction.

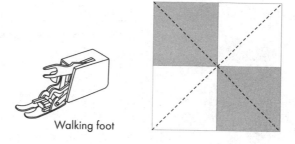

Walking foot

Use a walking foot for machine quilting straight lines.

A darning foot is used for free-motion quilting. The feed dogs are dropped and are nonfunctional when you do this type of quilting. You do not turn the quilt to change the direction of the stitching; you simply move the quilt as if you were drawing with the needle. Since you establish the length of the stitch by your motion and the sewing speed, this technique does take some practice.

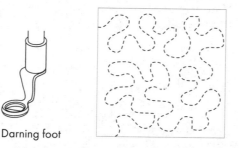

Darning foot

Use a darning foot for machine quilting free-motion lines.

Since your fingers need to move the fabric, wearing rubber gloves or those office rubber fingertips will help you do this. (Pssst....don't let anyone see you bringing the rubber gloves home. They might think you are planning to do some major housecleaning.)

Do not use hand-quilting thread to machine quilt. Most quilters use a lightweight cotton thread in the spool and bobbin. Some quilters use a transparent monofilament thread in the spool and bobbin. There are also many decorative threads available, and as you become more comfortable with machine quilting, you can experiment with these.

The good news is that these beginner projects are small, so they are perfect candidates for machine quilting. If this is your maiden voyage, I suggest you practice with straight-line designs and a walking foot until you are comfortable. Make a little practice square and play around with the stitch length and the feeling of machine quilting before you start on your project.

When you are ready to do the real thing, start in the middle of the project. Begin by stitching in place to lock in the beginning of your quilting line. Gradually increase the stitch length to about 10 stitches per inch.

I asked my friend Ellen Peters, who is an accomplished machine quilter, to offer some of her best machine-quilting tips for beginners. Ellen graciously offered the following:

1. A good clean machine is a must.
2. Use a new sewing machine needle for each project. Use the size needle appropriate for the thread you are using.
3. Use a good-quality thread. If you choose to machine quilt with transparent monofilament thread, buy one that is made specifically for machine quilting. If it acts like fishing line, don't use it.
4. When pin basting, place safety pins in areas where you will not be machine quilting so you won't have to move them.
5. Do all straight-line quilting with a walking foot first; then use a darning foot for free-motion quilting or fun sewing.
6. It takes practice to get free-motion quilting stitches even. Practice, practice, practice.

If you created your quilt top and are just tickled pink with the results, but aren't quite ready to jump in and hand or machine quilt your project, you do have other options.

Tying the three layers at regular intervals is one option. Sandwich the three layers as described earlier. Using a long needle and a single heavy thread, such as pearl cotton or yarn, stitch across the quilt as shown, spacing your stitches 6" to 8" apart. Cut the thread and tie a knot with the two ends. To make a secure knot, wrap the right thread over the left thread. Then wrap the left thread over the right thread twice and pull the ends. Trim the ends to about 1".

Having Options Is Neat

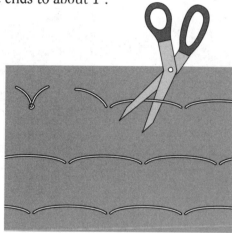

Another option is to have your quilt hand or machine quilted by a professional. Inquire at your local quilt shop or quilt guild about quilters who offer this service in your area. Machine quilting should be less expensive than hand quilting because it is less labor intensive.

Professional hand quilters will quilt in the design of your choice, or you can let them choose the design. Most machine quilters use a large commercial machine with computer-programmed patterns that create an allover design. You may be able to find a few machine quilters who do custom machine quilting, which is usually more expensive than programmed machine quilting.

Before giving your quilt top to someone for quilting, be sure you know exactly what services will be performed and how much it will cost. Some professional quilters expect the three layers to be already basted; others do not. Some will include binding the edges as part of the quilting fee; others will charge extra. Ask for references and take time to speak with previous customers.

Finishing Touches— Wow!

Can you believe it? You are ready to put the finishing touches on your quilt! I don't know what it is about the binding, but it gives such a crisp look to the quilt.

Binding: Finishing the Edge

Once you have completed the quilting or tying, it is time to bind the quilt. Prepare the quilt by removing the basting stitches or pins. Using a walking foot or the even-feed foot on your sewing machine, baste around the perimeter of the quilt, ⅛" from the edge. The walking foot helps sew all three layers smoothly. Use a rotary cutter and ruler to trim the batting and backing even with the edge of the quilt top. If you are adding a sleeve to hang your quilt, machine baste it in place now (see page 207).

Because the edges of wall quilts do not receive much stress from handling, I prefer to cut binding on the straight grain for wall quilts. Use straight-grain binding on straight edges only.

Make and Sew Straight-Grain Binding

1. To determine the length of binding required for your project, add 10" to the perimeter size.
2. Cut strips 2" wide across the width of the fabric (crosswise grain). Seam the ends at a 45° angle to make a strip long enough to go

around the outside edges of the quilt, plus about 10". Trim excess fabric, press seams open, and trim the points.

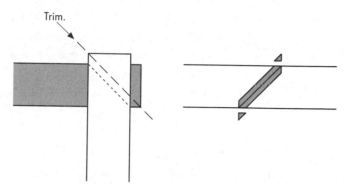

Trim.

3. Fold the strip in half lengthwise, wrong sides together, and press.

4. Place the binding on the front of the quilt, aligning the raw edges of the binding with the raw edges of the quilt. Use a walking foot to sew the binding to the quilt with a ¼"-wide seam. Leave the first few inches of the binding loose so you can join the beginning and ending of the binding strip later. Stop stitching ¼" from the corner of the quilt and backstitch.

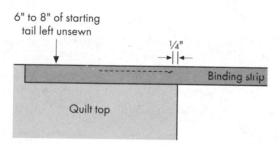

6" to 8" of starting
tail left unsewn

¼"

Binding strip

Quilt top

5. Turn the quilt to sew the next edge. Fold the binding up and away from the quilt and then down, even with the next side. The straight fold should be even with the top edge of the quilt. Stitch from the

edge to the next corner, stopping ¼" from the corner. Repeat for the remaining corners.

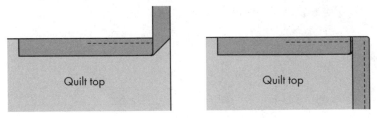

6. As you approach the beginning of the binding, stop and overlap the binding ½" from the start of the binding strip and trim excess. Open the folds of the two strips and sew the ends together with a ¼"-wide seam; press the seam allowance open. Return the seamed strip to the edge of the quilt and finish the seam.

7. Fold the binding to the back of the raw edges of the quilt, making sure to cover the machine stitching line. Use thread to match the color of the binding and a Sharp needle (type of needle, not a descriptive term about the point). Thread the needle with a single strand of sewing thread about 18" long; knot one end. Blindstitch the binding in place.

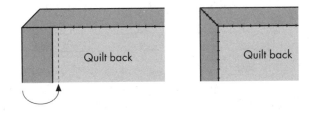

A blind stitch is a way of hand sewing an edge so that only tiny stitches are visible. Follow these easy steps to blindstitch the folded edge of the binding to the back of the quilt.

1. Insert the threaded needle under the edge of the binding, close to the fold.

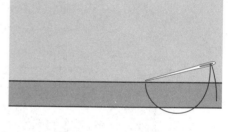

2. Insert the needle directly across from where it went into the binding, into the backing and batting only. Place your other hand under the edge of the quilt top so you can make sure the needle does not go through the top. Your fingers will alert you if the needle comes through. You don't want to see the stitches on the front of the quilt.

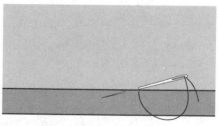

3. Slide the needle under the backing and batting about an ⅛", then bring it up through the backing into the folded edge of the binding. Repeat from step 2 until you near the end of the thread.

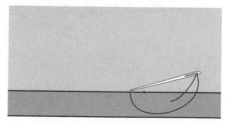

4. To end the thread, take 2 or 3 stitches in the same place along the edge of the binding. Slide the needle through the binding to hide the end of the thread and cut.

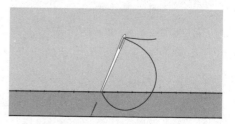

Since I love charts, the following chart will tell you approximately how much 2"-wide straight-grain binding can be cut from 44"-wide yardage.

2"-Wide Straight-Grain Binding				
¼ yd.	4 strips x 44"	=	176"
⅓ yd.	6 strips x 44"	=	264"
½ yd.	9 strips x 44"	=	396"

Make and Sew Bias-Grain Binding

I use fabric strips cut on the bias when binding bed quilts because bias strips are stronger and more durable. You can use bias bindings on straight or curved edges.

1. To cut bias strips, fold a fabric square in half diagonally and press. Fold the square diagonally a second time.

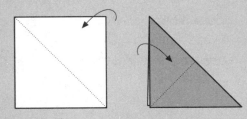

Two folds

2. Make a clean cut to remove the two folds. Cut 2"-wide strips and join them as shown with a ¼"-wide seam.

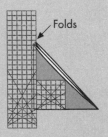

Folds

Remove both folds.

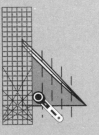

Cut bias strips.

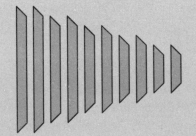

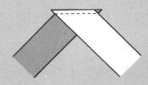

Join the bias strips.

3. Press under ¼" at one end. Fold the strip in half lengthwise, wrong sides together, and press.

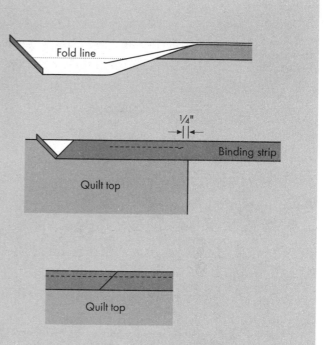

4. Sew the binding and treat the corners as described in straight-grain binding, steps 4 and 5, on pages 201–202.

5. As you approach the beginning of the binding, stop and overlap the binding with the start of the binding strip. Open the fold and trim the excess. Return the trimmed strip to the edge, slip it inside the beginning, and finish the seam.

6. Finish as described in straight-grain binding, step 7, on page 202.

To determine the approximate length of 2"-wide bias strips that can be cut from a square, divide the size of the square by 2" and multiply your answer by the size of the square. For example, a 20" square divided by 2 equals ten. Ten times 20 equals 200. Therefore, a 20" square will yield approximately 200" of 2"-wide bias binding. Remember, this does not take into account seams, so it is only an approximation. The following chart will tell you approximately how much 2"-wide bias-grain binding can be cut from a particular size square.

SIZE OF SQUARE	LENGTH OF 2"-WIDE BIAS BINDING
18"	162"
20"	200"
24"	288"
26"	338"
28"	392"
30"	450"

No-Corners Option

If you don't want to deal with the corners of your project, you don't have to. You have the option of eliminating them by rounding them off. Place a dinner plate across the corner of your project and rotary cut a gentle curve.

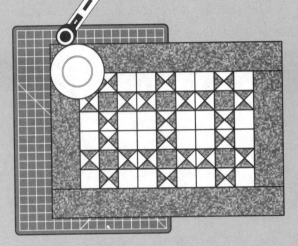
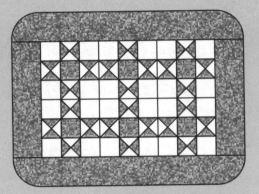

You must use bias-grain binding so it will stretch around the corner. Attach the binding as described earlier, except place and sew the bias binding gently around the curve.

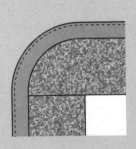
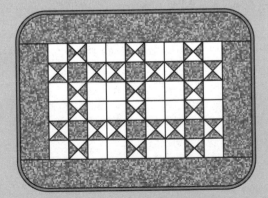

To avoid putting stress on your quilt as it hangs on a wall, it is best to slip a rod through a sleeve sewn on the back of the quilt. You can use the same fabric as the backing for the sleeve so it will blend in, or simply a piece of muslin. You can add a sleeve after you've sewn on the binding, but attaching it before you bind it is efficient, and stitching the sleeve to all three layers of the top provides better support for the quilt.

Adding a Sleeve

1. Cut a strip of fabric as long as the width of the quilt and double the desired width of the sleeve plus ½" for seam allowance. Turn under ¼" twice at each end to hem both ends of the strip.

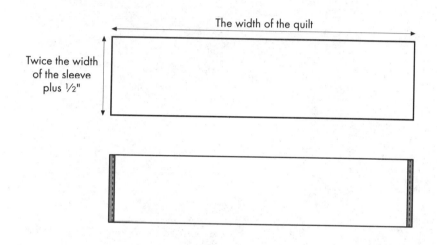

The width of the quilt

Twice the width of the sleeve plus ½"

2. Fold the strip, wrong sides together, and pin the raw edges at the top of the quilt before you attach the binding. Machine baste in place, ⅛" from the top edge. Add the binding to the quilt as described on pages 201–202.

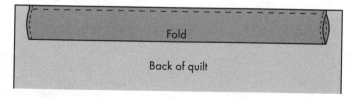

Fold

Back of quilt

3. Blindstitch the folded edge of the sleeve to the back of the quilt. Be careful not to stitch through to the front of the quilt.

Leaving Your Signature

Your quilt is an expression of you. Be sure to make a label for the back of the quilt containing information such as your name, the date the quilt was completed, the name of the quilt, your city and state, the recipient if it is a gift, and any other information you would like to add. You can write this information on a piece of fabric with a permanent pen or make a more elaborate stitched label.

Parting Thoughts

Although a quilt is your ultimate goal, take time to enjoy the different processes along the way. Feel the excitement of selecting your first project. Enjoy choosing fabrics and colors you really like. Marvel at the accomplishment of cutting fabrics into pieces that will make a design statement. Feel the fulfillment of adding your particular stamp to the quilting designs. Relax as you get caught up in the rhythm of hand or machine quilting. Smile at the finished quilt crafted by your hands that contains a bit of you!

Quilting does not need to be a solitary art. You'll be amazed at how many quilters there are all over the world. Wherever there are quilters, they gather at quilt guilds to share their love of quilting and support each other. Show-and-tell is often a favorite time of their regular meetings, where a first quilt is applauded and appreciated as much as any other.

Quilt shows, held at the local and national levels, display quilts to encourage and inspire. There are quilt magazines that also inspire, inform, and teach. You can continue to grow in your quilting by taking classes through adult-education programs and at your local quilt shop. If you are connected to the information superhighway, you'll find computer quilt forums where you can correspond with quilters worldwide. And I'm happy to announce that I'm working with several authors to bring you a series of books covering additional basic quiltmaking techniques that build on the knowledge you found in this book. To whet your appetite, hand appliqué and strip piecing are just two subjects planned for the near future.

The quilting community is a sharing and nurturing one. All quilters were beginning quilters once and can remember a time when they, too, were clueless. Let me be one of the first to welcome you to the wonderful world of quilting, and may your first experiences and those down the road be fun and fulfilling.

Templates

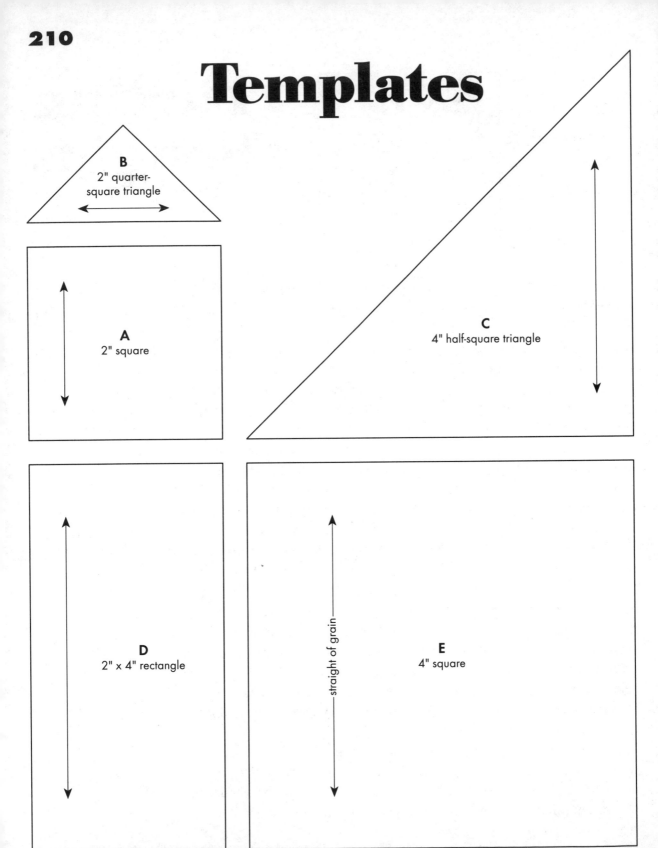

B
2" quarter-
square triangle

A
2" square

C
4" half-square triangle

D
2" x 4" rectangle

straight of grain

E
4" square

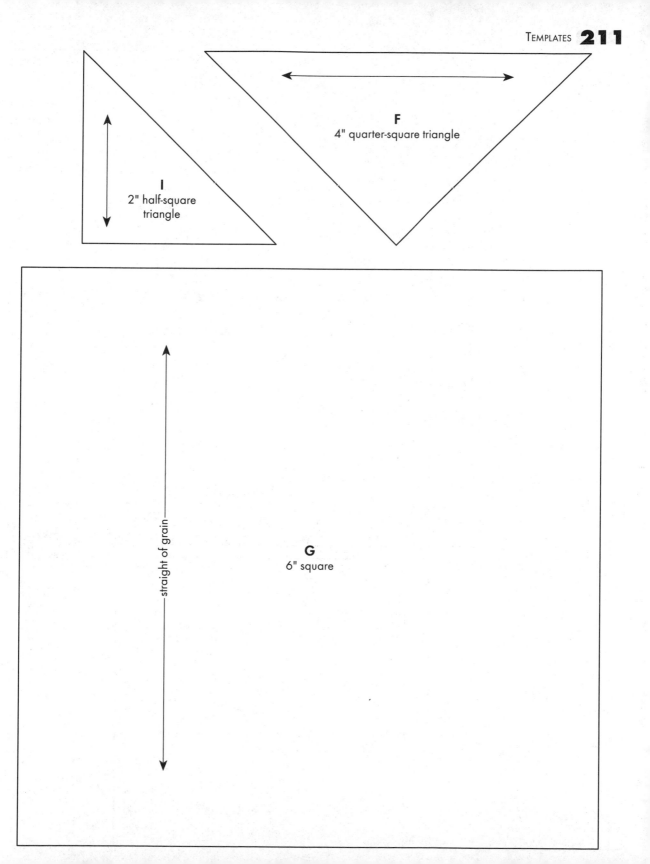

F
4" quarter-square triangle

I
2" half-square
triangle

G
6" square

straight of grain

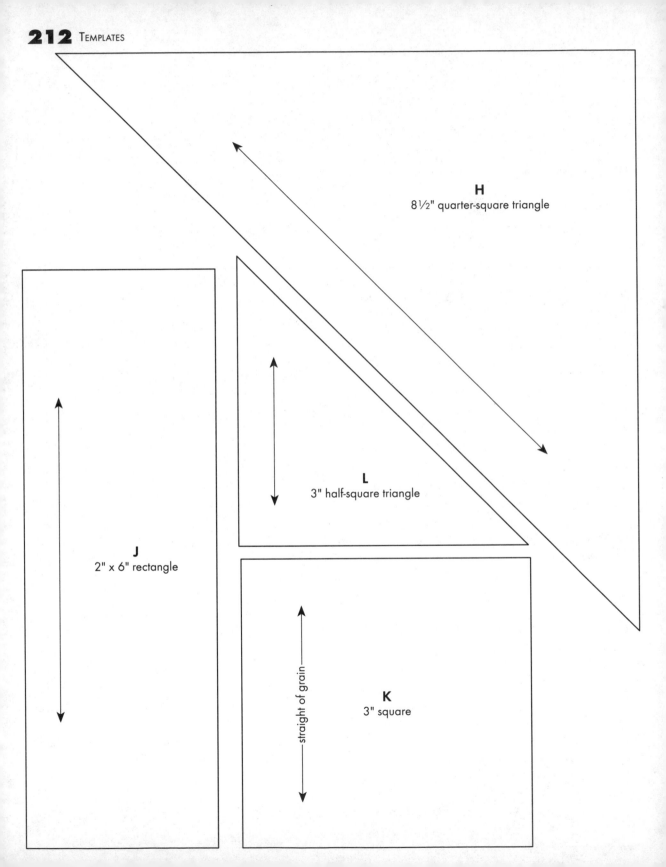

H
8½" quarter-square triangle

L
3" half-square triangle

J
2" x 6" rectangle

K
3" square

straight of grain

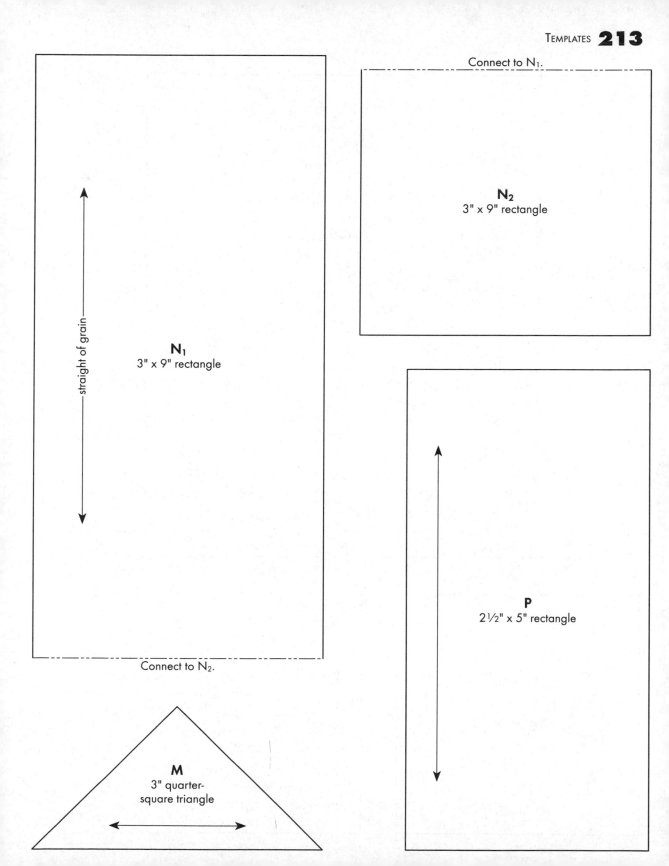

Connect to N₁.

N₂
3" x 9" rectangle

straight of grain

N₁
3" x 9" rectangle

Connect to N₂.

P
2½" x 5" rectangle

M
3" quarter-
square triangle

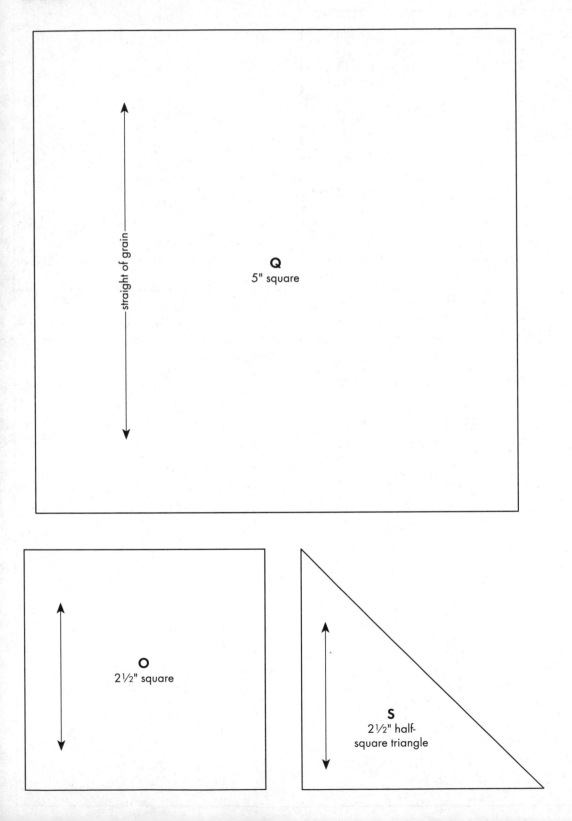

straight of grain

Q
5" square

O
2½" square

S
2½" half-
square triangle

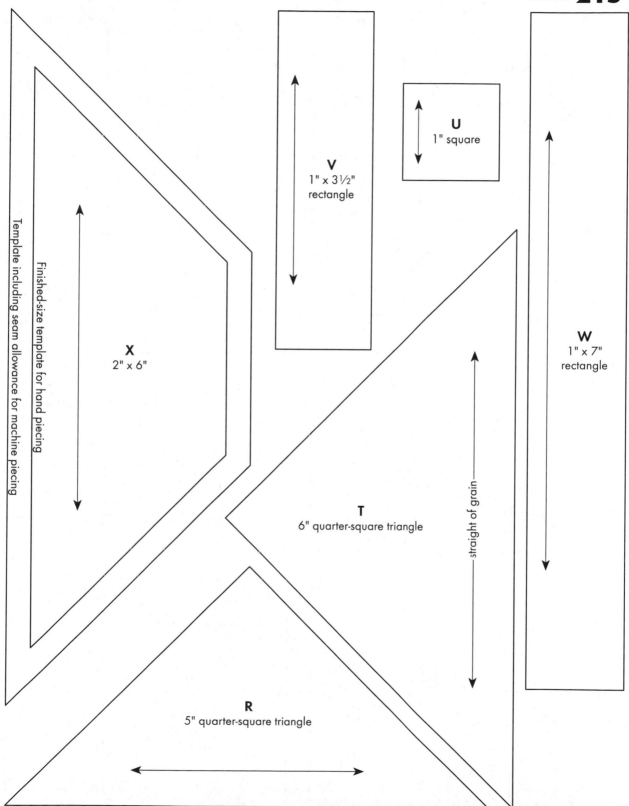

Template including seam allowance for machine piecing

Finished-size template for hand piecing

X
2" x 6"

V
1" x 3½"
rectangle

U
1" square

W
1" x 7"
rectangle

straight of grain

T
6" quarter-square triangle

R
5" quarter-square triangle

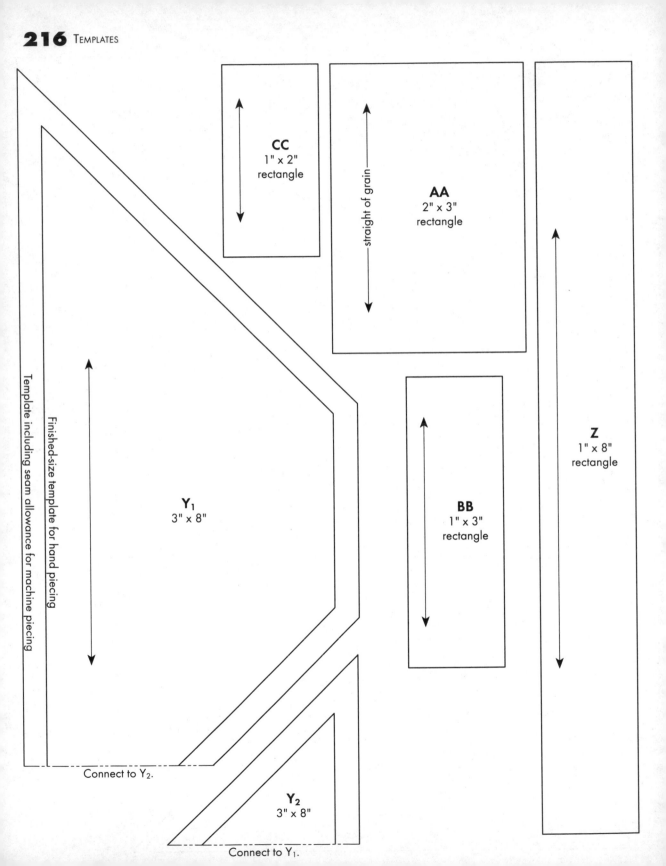

CC
1" x 2"
rectangle

straight of grain

AA
2" x 3"
rectangle

Z
1" x 8"
rectangle

Template including seam allowance for machine piecing

Finished-size template for hand piecing

Y₁
3" x 8"

BB
1" x 3"
rectangle

Connect to Y₂.

Y₂
3" x 8"

Connect to Y₁.

Quilting Designs

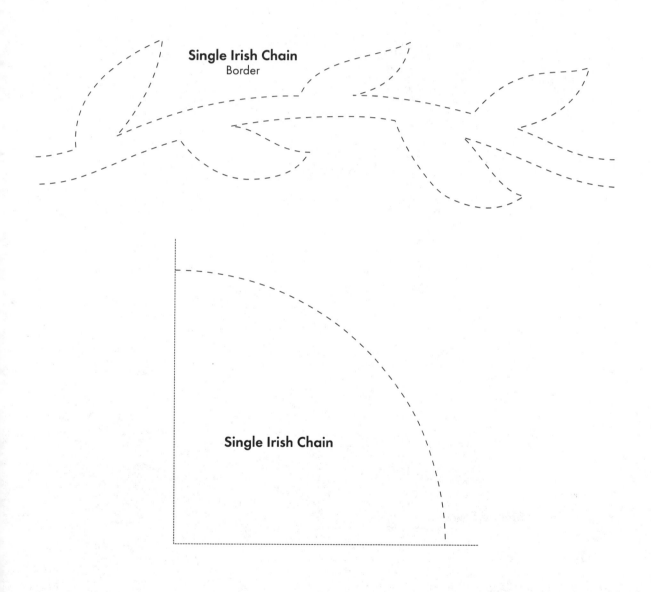

Single Irish Chain
Border

Single Irish Chain

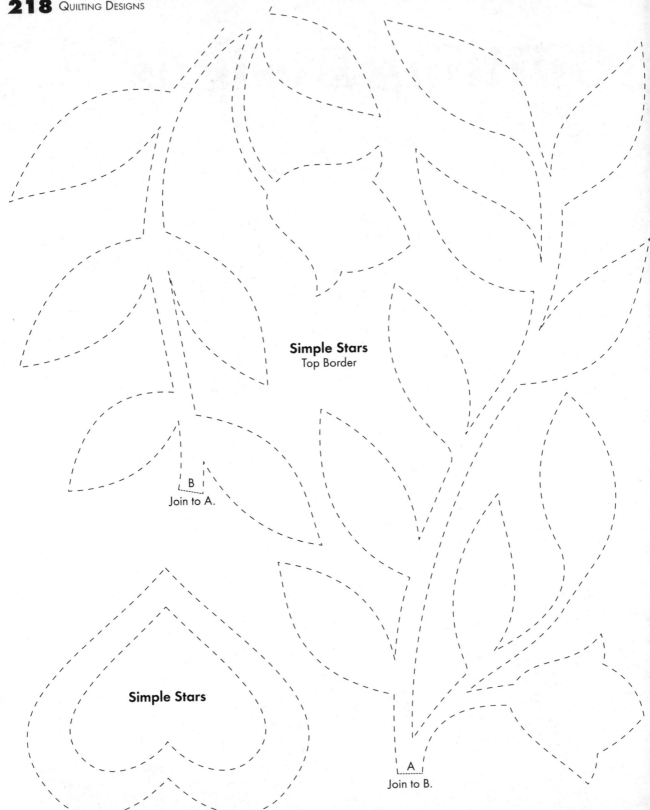

Simple Stars
Top Border

B
Join to A.

Simple Stars

A
Join to B.

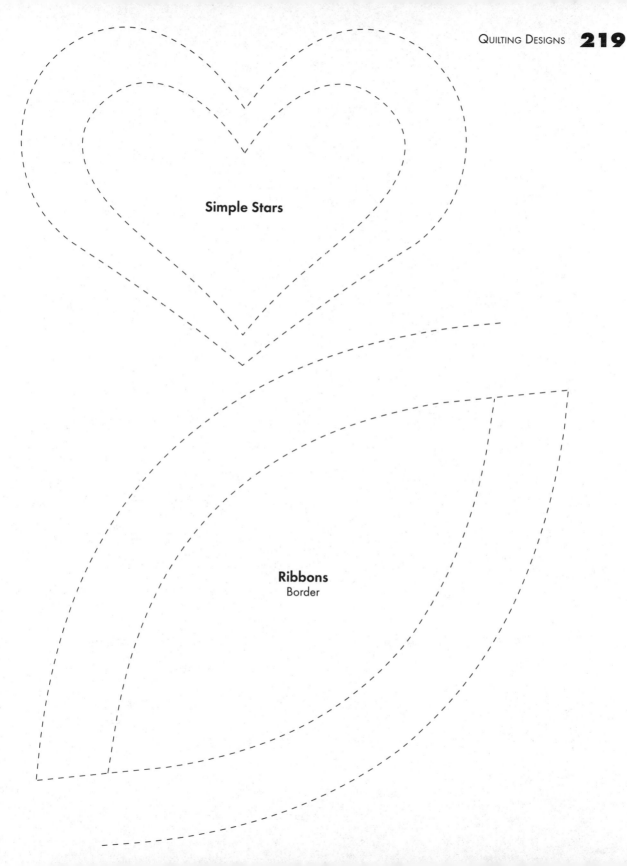

Simple Stars

Ribbons
Border

Simple Stars

Simple Stars

Star Bright

Simple Stars

Suggested Books

General Quiltmaking Techniques

The Joy of Quilting by Joan Hanson and Mary Hickey (That Patchwork Place)

Quiltmaker's Guide: Basics & Beyond by Carol Doak (American Quilter's Society)

Patchwork Block Designs (Block Dictionary)

Encyclopedia of Pieced Quilt Patterns, compiled by Barbara Brackman (American Quilter's Society)

Patchwork Patterns by Jinny Beyer (EPM Publications, Inc.)

The Quilter's Album of Blocks & Borders by Jinny Beyer (EPM Publications, Inc.)

Color

Color: The Quilter's Guide by Christine Barnes (That Patchwork Place)

Color & Cloth by Mary Coyne Penders (The Quilt Digest Press)

Rotary-Cut and Machine-Sewn Patchwork

Around the Block with Judy Hopkins (That Patchwork Place)

Shortcuts by Donna Lynn Thomas (That Patchwork Place)

A Perfect Match by Donna Lynn Thomas (That Patchwork Place)

Appliqué

Appliqué: 12 Easy Ways by Elly Sienkiewicz (C & T Publishing)

The Easy Art of Appliqué by Mimi Dietrich and Roxi Eppler (That Patchwork Place)

Hand Quilting

How to Improve Your Quilting Stitch by Ami Simms (Mallery Press)

Loving Stitches by Jeana Kimball (That Patchwork Place)

Machine Quilting

Machine Quilting Made Easy by Maurine Noble (That Patchwork Place)

Heirloom Machine Quilting by Harriet Hargrave (C & T Publishing)

Quilting Designs

Quilting Makes the Quilt by Lee Cleland (That Patchwork Place)

Quilting Design Sourcebook by Dorothy Osler (That Patchwork Place)

Bindings or Edge Treatments

Happy Endings by Mimi Dietrich (That Patchwork Place)

A Fine Finish by Cody Mazuran (That Patchwork Place)

Informational Charts

Taking the Math Out of Making Patchwork Quilts by Bonnie Leman & Judy Martin (Leman Publications, Inc.)

Bibliography

Beyer, Jinny. *Patchwork Patterns.* McLean, Va.: EPM Publications, 1979.

———. *The Quilter's Album of Blocks & Borders.* McLean, Va.: EPM Publications, 1980.

Brackman, Barbara. *Encyclopedia of Pieced Quilt Patterns.* Paducah, Ky.: American Quilter's Society, 1993.

Doak, Carol. *Quiltmaker's Guide: Basics & Beyond.* Paducah, Ky.: American Quilter's Society, 1992.

———. *Country Medallion Sampler.* Bothell, Wash.: That Patchwork Place, Inc., 1993.

———. *Easy Machine Paper Piecing.* Bothell, Wash.: That Patchwork Place, Inc., 1994.

Hanson, Joan. *Sensational Settings.* Bothell, Wash.: That Patchwork Place, Inc., 1993.

Hanson, Joan, and Mary Hickey. *The Joy of Quilting.* Bothell, Wash.: That Patchwork Place, Inc., 1995.

Martin, Nancy J. *Fun with Fat Quarters.* Bothell, Wash.: That Patchwork Place, Inc., 1994.

Noble, Maurine. *Machine Quilting Made Easy.* Bothell, Wash.: That Patchwork Place, Inc., 1994.

Rehmel, Judy. *The Quilt I.D. Book.* New York: Prentice Hall Press, 1986.

Index

About the Author

Carol Doak is an award-winning quiltmaker as well as a popular teacher and best-selling author. She has made more than one hundred fifty quilts since taking her first quiltmaking class in Worthington, Ohio. Carol began teaching beginning quiltmakers in 1980 through an adult-education quilting class and continued to teach this comprehensive class for several years in local quilt shops. She currently travels internationally to share her quiltmaking "Tricks of the Trade." Her lighthearted approach and ability to teach beginners as well as more advanced quilters have earned her high marks and positive comments from workshop participants wherever she travels.

Carol's Blue Ribbon quilts have appeared in several books, including *Great American Quilts 1990* and *The Quilt Encyclopedia,* and on the covers of *Quilter's Newsletter Magazine, Quilt World, Quilting Today, McCall's Quilting,* and *Lady's Circle Patchwork Quilts.*

Carol's students encouraged her to write her first book in 1992. Since then, Carol has written eight more books and is working on another one!

Carol lives with her family in Windham, New Hampshire. She claims the cold winters give her plenty of reason to stockpile fabric, since it offers insulation as well as gratification.

Books by Carol Doak

Comical Country Sampler (House of White Birches, Inc., 1995)

Easy Machine Paper Piecing (That Patchwork Place, 1993)

Easy Mix & Match Machine Paper Piecing (That Patchwork Place, 1995)

Easy Paper-Pieced Keepsake Quilts (That Patchwork Place, 1995)

Easy Reversible Vests (That Patchwork Place, 1995)

Quiltmaker's Guide: Basics and Beyond (American Quilter's Society, 1992)

Show Me How to Paper Piece (That Patchwork Place, 1997)

Notes

Notes

new and bestselling titles from

America's Best-Loved Craft & Hobby Books™

America's Best-Loved Quilt Books®

NEW RELEASES
1000 Great Quilt Blocks
American Stenciled Quilts
Americana Quilts
Appliquilt in the Cabin
Bed and Breakfast Quilts
Best of Black Mountain Quilts, The
Beyond the Blocks
Blissful Bath, The
Celebrations!
Color-Blend Appliqué
Fabulous Quilts from Favorite Patterns
Feathers That Fly
Handcrafted Garden Accents
Handprint Quilts
Knitted Throws and More for the Simply
    Beautiful Home
Knitter's Book of Finishing Techniques, The
Knitter's Template, A
Make Room for Christmas Quilts
More Paintbox Knits
Painted Whimsies
Patriotic Little Quilts
Quick Quilts Using Quick Bias
Quick-Change Quilts
Quilts for Mantels and More
Snuggle Up
Split-Diamond Dazzlers
Stack the Deck!
Strips and Strings
Sweet Dreams
Treasury of Rowan Knits, A
Triangle Tricks
Triangle-Free Quilts

APPLIQUÉ
Artful Album Quilts
Artful Appliqué
Blossoms in Winter
Easy Art of Appliqué, The
Fun with Sunbonnet Sue
Sunbonnet Sue All through the Year

BABY QUILTS
Easy Paper-Pieced Baby Quilts
Even More Quilts for Baby
More Quilts for Baby
Play Quilts
Quilted Nursery, The
Quilts for Baby

HOLIDAY QUILTS
Christmas at That Patchwork Place®
Christmas Cats and Dogs
Creepy Crafty Halloween
Handcrafted Christmas, A
Welcome to the North Pole

LEARNING TO QUILT
Joy of Quilting, The
Nickel Quilts
Quick Watercolor Quilts
Quilts from Aunt Amy
Simple Joys of Quilting, The
Your First Quilt Book (or it should be!)

PAPER PIECING
40 Bright and Bold Paper-Pieced Blocks
50 Fabulous Paper-Pieced Stars
For the Birds
Quilter's Ark, A
Rich Traditions

ROTARY CUTTING
101 Fabulous Rotary-Cut Quilts
365 Quilt Blocks a Year Perpetual Calendar
Around the Block Again
Around the Block with Judy Hopkins
Log Cabin Fever
More Fat Quarter Quilts

TOPICS IN QUILTMAKING
Batik Beauties
Frayed-Edge Fun
Log Cabin Fever
Machine Quilting Made Easy
Quick Watercolor Quilts
Reversible Quilts

CRAFTS
300 Papermaking Recipes
ABCs of Making Teddy Bears, The
Creating with Paint
Handcrafted Frames
Painted Chairs
Stamp in Color
Stamp with Style

KNITTING & CROCHET
365 Knitting Stitches a Year Perpetual
    Calendar
Clever Knits
Crochet for Babies and Toddlers
Crocheted Sweaters
Irresistible Knits
Knitted Shawls, Stoles, and Scarves
Knitted Sweaters for Every Season
Knitting with Novelty Yarns
Paintbox Knits
Simply Beautiful Sweaters
Simply Beautiful Sweaters for Men
Too Cute! Cotton Knits for Toddlers
Ultimate Knitter's Guide, The

Our books are available at bookstores and your favorite craft, fabric, and yarn
retailers. If you don't see the title you're looking for, visit us at
www.martingale-pub.com or contact us at:

1-800-426-3126

International: 1-425-483-3313

Fax: 1-425-486-7596

E-mail: info@martingale-pub.com

For more information and a full list of our titles, visit our Web site.